The Manifestation Blueprint

The Manifestation Blueprint

Transform Your Life with the Power Within

Eathan Rivers

Mindful Pages

Published in 2024

ISBN: 9789358814682 (PB)
ISBN: 9789358815221 (eBook)

Published by

Mindful Pages
Imprint of Alpha Editions LLC
312 W. 2nd St #1834
Casper, WY 82601, USA
www.mindfulpagespublishers.com

Contents

Introduction

Welcome to "The Manifestation Blueprint: Transform Your Life with the Power Within." In the pages that follow, you will embark on a journey of self-discovery, empowerment, and transformation. This book is not just about wishful thinking or dreaming big; it's about understanding and harnessing the extraordinary power of manifestation to create the life you desire.

But what exactly is manifestation, and why is it so important? Manifestation is the process of bringing your thoughts, beliefs, and desires into reality. It's about consciously creating the life you want by aligning your thoughts, emotions, and actions with your deepest desires and intentions. At its core, manifestation is the belief that we have the power to shape our reality through our thoughts and actions.

The importance of manifestation cannot be overstated. In a world filled with uncertainty and challenges, it offers us a beacon of hope and empowerment. By learning to harness the power of manifestation, we can break free from limiting beliefs, overcome obstacles, and create the life of our dreams.

Manifestation is not a new concept; it has been practiced for centuries by cultures around the world. However, in recent years, it has gained renewed attention thanks to books like "The Secret" and the rise of the Law of Attraction movement. While these teachings have brought manifestation into the mainstream, they often oversimplify the process, leaving many feeling frustrated and disillusioned.

That's where this book comes in. "The Manifestation Blueprint" is not just another self-help book; it's a comprehensive guide that will take you step-by-step through the process of manifestation, providing you with practical tools, exercises, and techniques to help you unlock your full potential.

Throughout these pages, you will learn how to:

> Cultivate self-awareness and clarity about your goals and desires.

Identify and release self-limiting beliefs that are holding you back.

Harness the power of visualization and affirmations to reprogram your subconscious mind.

Take inspired action towards your goals with confidence and purpose.

Practice detachment and trust in the universe to manifest your desires effortlessly.

Overcome obstacles and setbacks with resilience and determination.

Manifest abundance, success, and fulfilment in all areas of your life.

But perhaps most importantly, you will learn that manifestation is not just about getting what you want; it's about becoming who you were meant to be. It's about tapping into your inner wisdom, aligning with your true purpose, and living a life of passion, joy, and fulfilment.

So are you ready to embark on this transformative journey? Are you ready to unlock the power within you and manifest the life of your dreams? If so, then let's begin. The manifestation blueprint awaits, and your destiny beckons.

Setting the Purpose and Goals: Unveiling "The Manifestation Blueprint

In a world inundated with self-help books promising overnight success and instant transformation, it's easy to become skeptical of yet another guide claiming to hold the key to unlocking one's full potential. However, "The Manifestation Blueprint" is not just another addition to the crowded genre of self-help literature; it is a meticulously crafted roadmap designed to guide you on a journey of profound self-discovery and empowerment.

Understanding the Purpose:

At its core, the purpose of "The Manifestation Blueprint" is to empower you to become the architect of your own destiny. It seeks to unravel the mysteries of manifestation and provide you with practical tools and strategies to harness the power within you to create the life you desire.

But what sets this book apart from the countless others on manifestation and personal development? The answer lies in its holistic approach and unwavering commitment to authenticity and depth. Rather than offering quick fixes or empty promises, "The Manifestation Blueprint" delves deep into the underlying principles of manifestation, guiding you through a transformative process that encompasses mind, body, and spirit.

Exploring the Goals:

As you embark on your journey through "The Manifestation Blueprint," you will encounter a series of goals that will serve as beacons of light illuminating your path forward:

> **Self-Discovery:** The first goal of this book is to help you cultivate a deep sense of self-awareness and clarity about your goals, desires, and values. Through reflective exercises and introspective practices, you will uncover hidden truths about yourself and gain insights that will serve as the foundation for your manifestation journey.

> **Empowerment:** Armed with self-awareness, you will be empowered to challenge and transcend the self-limiting beliefs and negative thought patterns that have been holding you back. Through practical techniques such as visualization, affirmations, and positive self-talk, you will learn to reprogram your subconscious mind and unleash your full potential.

> **Action:** Manifestation is not just about wishing and waiting for your desires to magically materialize; it requires decisive action and unwavering commitment. Throughout this book, you will be encouraged to take inspired action towards your goals, stepping out of your comfort zone and embracing new opportunities with courage and confidence.

> **Alignment:** Central to the manifestation process is the concept of alignment – aligning your thoughts, emotions, and actions with your deepest desires and intentions. Through mindfulness practices and intentional living, you will learn to cultivate a state of inner harmony and resonance that will magnetize your desires to you effortlessly.

Fulfilment: Ultimately, the goal of "The Manifestation Blueprint" is to guide you towards a life of deep fulfilment, purpose, and meaning. By aligning with your true purpose and living in alignment with your values, you will experience a profound sense of joy and satisfaction that transcends material success.

Understanding the Blueprint Concept:

At the heart of "The Manifestation Blueprint" lies a powerful metaphor – the blueprint. Just as a blueprint serves as a detailed plan for constructing a building, this book serves as a blueprint for constructing the life of your dreams. Each chapter is carefully crafted to build upon the next, guiding you through a step-by-step process of self-discovery, empowerment, and transformation.

Just as a blueprint provides structure and direction, "The Manifestation Blueprint" provides you with the guidance and support you need to navigate the often challenging terrain of personal growth and development. Whether you're a seasoned manifestor or a newcomer to the world of manifestation, this book will meet you wherever you are on your journey and provide you with the tools and insights you need to take the next steps forward.

In the pages that follow, you will find a treasure trove of wisdom, inspiration, and practical guidance that will empower you to become the architect of your own destiny. So, are you ready to embark on this transformative journey? Are you ready to unlock the power within you and manifest the life of your dreams? If so, then let the journey begin. The manifestation blueprint awaits, and your destiny beckons.

Chapter 1: The Fundamentals of Manifestation

In this foundational chapter, we will delve into the fundamental principles of manifestation, laying the groundwork for your journey of self-discovery and empowerment. Manifestation is not just a mystical concept reserved for the enlightened few; it is a natural and inherent ability that each of us possesses. By understanding and mastering these fundamentals, you will gain the tools and insights you need to harness the power of manifestation and create the life you desire.

At its core, manifestation is the process of bringing your thoughts, beliefs, and desires into reality. It is based on the principle that like attracts like – in other words, the energy you put out into the universe is reflected back to you in the form of your experiences and circumstances. Manifestation is not about wishful thinking or passive waiting; it is an active and intentional process that requires clarity, focus, and alignment.

Central to the concept of manifestation is the Law of Attraction, which states that like attracts like. According to this law, your thoughts and emotions have a magnetic quality that attracts similar energy vibrations into your life. In other words, if you focus on positive thoughts and emotions, you will attract positive experiences and opportunities into your life, whereas if you dwell on negativity and lack, you will attract more of the same.

Your thoughts and beliefs shape your reality more than you may realize. The thoughts you consistently hold in your mind create a blueprint for your experiences, shaping the way you perceive and interact with the world around you. By becoming aware of your thoughts and beliefs and consciously choosing to focus on those that align with your desires, you can begin to reshape your reality from the inside out.

Two powerful tools for manifestation are visualization and affirmations. Visualization involves mentally picturing yourself experiencing your desired outcomes in vivid detail, engaging all of your senses to create a sense of immersion and reality. Affirmations are positive statements that you repeat to yourself regularly to reinforce positive beliefs and intentions. When used consistently and with intention, these practices can help to reprogram your subconscious mind and align your thoughts and beliefs with your desires.

As we embark on this journey of exploration and discovery, it's important to remember that manifestation is not a one-size-fits-all process. What works for one person may not work for another, and it's essential to find the techniques and practices that resonate most deeply with you. In the chapters that follow, we will delve deeper into the principles of manifestation and explore practical exercises and techniques to help you harness the power of manifestation and create the life you desire. So, are you ready to unlock the secrets of manifestation and transform your life from the inside out? If so, let's dive in. The journey awaits, and the possibilities are limitless.

Define Manifestation and Its Principles

Manifestation, often hailed as a mystical force or esoteric concept, is fundamentally the art of bringing your thoughts, beliefs, and desires into tangible reality. It's about consciously co-creating the life you envision by aligning your thoughts, emotions, and actions with your deepest intentions. While it may seem like a fantastical notion reserved for the spiritually enlightened, manifestation is, in fact, a natural and inherent ability that each of us possesses.

At its essence, manifestation operates on the principle that the energy we emit into the universe attracts similar energy vibrations back to us—a concept often referred to as the Law of Attraction. This universal law posits that like attracts like, meaning that the thoughts, emotions, and beliefs we consistently hold shape our external experiences and circumstances. In other words, the more we focus on positive thoughts and feelings, the more positivity we draw into our lives, while dwelling on negativity tends to attract more of the same.

Central to the concept of manifestation are several key principles that underpin its practice:

> **Clarity of Intentions:** Manifestation begins with a clear understanding of what you want to manifest. This involves

identifying your goals, desires, and aspirations with precision and clarity. The more specific and detailed your intentions, the easier it becomes to align your thoughts and actions with them.

Positive Visualization: Visualization is a powerful technique used to mentally create and experience desired outcomes. By vividly imagining yourself achieving your goals and experiencing the associated emotions, you reinforce your belief in their attainment and signal to the universe your readiness to receive.

Affirmations and Positive Self-Talk: Affirmations are positive statements that you repeat to yourself regularly to reinforce empowering beliefs and intentions. By affirming what you want as if it's already happening, you reprogram your subconscious mind and align your thoughts with your desires.

Emotional Alignment: Emotions serve as powerful indicators of alignment with your desires. When you feel joy, excitement, and gratitude for your envisioned outcomes, you signal to the universe your readiness to receive. Conversely, negative emotions such as doubt, fear, and lack can create resistance and hinder the manifestation process.

Taking Inspired Action: While manifestation involves aligning with the flow of the universe, it also requires taking decisive action towards your goals. Inspired action is action taken from a place of alignment and intuition, guided by inner wisdom and purpose.

Detachment and Trust: Manifestation is about striking a delicate balance between intention and surrender, effort and detachment. Detachment involves letting go of attachment to specific outcomes and trusting in the universe's timing and wisdom. It's about releasing the need to control every aspect of the manifestation process and surrendering to the flow of life.

By embracing these principles and integrating them into your daily life, you can unlock the transformative power of manifestation and create the life of your dreams. Manifestation is not about wishful thinking or passive waiting; it's about becoming an active participant in the creation of your reality. So, dare to dream big, align your thoughts with your desires, and trust in the inherent power within you to manifest your deepest aspirations. The universe is conspiring in your favor—now it's time to harness its limitless potential.

Unveiling the Law of Attraction: A Key Element of Manifestation

The Law of Attraction stands as a cornerstone principle in the realm of manifestation, offering insights into the interconnectedness between our thoughts, emotions, and external reality. While its roots trace back through centuries of philosophical and spiritual teachings, it gained widespread attention in recent decades, particularly with the advent of books like "The Secret" and the burgeoning popularity of the New Thought movement.

At its core, the Law of Attraction posits that like attracts like. In other words, the energy we emit—through our thoughts, beliefs, and emotions—draws corresponding experiences and circumstances into our lives. This universal principle implies that our reality is not merely a product of external forces or random chance but is intricately shaped by the vibrational frequency we emit into the cosmos.

The Law of Attraction and manifestation share a symbiotic relationship, with the former serving as a guiding principle underlying the latter's practice. Manifestation involves the deliberate alignment of one's thoughts, beliefs, and intentions with desired outcomes, thereby harnessing the Law of Attraction to bring those desires into fruition.

When you focus your attention on positive thoughts and emotions, you raise your vibrational frequency, thereby attracting similar high-vibrational experiences into your life. Conversely, dwelling on negativity or lack tends to perpetuate a cycle of attracting undesirable circumstances.

Manifestation operates most effectively when there is alignment between your thoughts, emotions, and intentions. By cultivating a mindset of abundance, gratitude, and positivity, you create a fertile ground for manifestation to occur. When your thoughts and beliefs are congruent with your desired outcomes, you signal to the universe your readiness to receive.

Practicing manifestation involves actively shaping your thoughts and beliefs to align with your goals and desires. Visualization, affirmations, and gratitude practices serve as powerful tools for reinforcing positive intentions and imprinting them onto your subconscious mind. By consistently engaging in these practices and maintaining a state of emotional alignment, you enhance your receptivity to the abundance that surrounds you.

While the Law of Attraction emphasizes the power of thoughts and beliefs, it's essential to recognize that manifestation also requires inspired action. Taking proactive steps towards your goals not only demonstrates your commitment and dedication but also sends a clear signal to the universe of your readiness to manifest your desires.

In essence, the Law of Attraction serves as a guiding principle that underscores the transformative potential of manifestation. By understanding and harnessing this universal law, you unlock the power to consciously create the life you desire. As you embark on your journey of manifestation, remember that your thoughts are the building blocks of your reality—so dare to dream big, align your intentions with your desires, and watch as the universe conspires to bring your aspirations to life.

Unleashing the Power of Thoughts and Beliefs

In the intricate dance of manifestation, thoughts and beliefs stand as the architects of our reality, shaping the landscape of our experiences and directing the course of our lives. Understanding and harnessing the power of these mental constructs is crucial to unlocking the full potential of manifestation.

Thoughts are the silent whispers that echo through the corridors of our minds, shaping our perceptions, attitudes, and actions. They possess an immense creative potential, capable of birthing both dreams and nightmares into existence. Every thought we entertain sends ripples of energy into the universe, setting in motion a chain reaction of events and circumstances that align with its vibrational frequency.

Beliefs, on the other hand, serve as the bedrock upon which our reality is constructed. They are the deeply ingrained convictions that govern our perceptions of ourselves, others, and the world around us. Whether consciously acknowledged or buried deep within the subconscious, our beliefs act as potent filters through which we interpret our experiences and navigate the complexities of life.

Central to the power of thoughts and beliefs is the subconscious mind—a vast reservoir of memories, emotions, and programming that operates beneath the surface of conscious awareness. It is within this hidden realm that our deepest desires, fears, and aspirations reside, exerting a profound influence on our thoughts, behaviors, and manifestations.

In the realm of manifestation, thoughts and beliefs serve as the cornerstone principles upon which the process unfolds. Every thought we entertain, every belief we hold, sends out energetic signals that attract corresponding experiences into our lives. Positive thoughts and empowering beliefs act as magnets, drawing forth abundance, joy, and fulfilment, while negative thoughts and limiting beliefs repel the very blessings we seek to manifest.

To harness the power of thoughts and beliefs for manifestation, it is essential to engage in the deliberate process of reprogramming the subconscious mind. This involves identifying and challenging ingrained patterns of thought and belief that no longer serve our highest good, replacing them with new, empowering narratives aligned with our desires and aspirations.

Various techniques and practices can aid in the reprogramming of the mind, including visualization, affirmations, and mindfulness. Visualization allows us to vividly imagine our desired outcomes, imprinting them onto the subconscious mind with clarity and conviction. Affirmations serve as powerful statements of intent, reinforcing positive beliefs and intentions at a subconscious level. Mindfulness cultivates awareness of our thoughts and beliefs, enabling us to recognize and release patterns of negativity and limitation.

In the tapestry of manifestation, thoughts and beliefs emerge as the threads that weave together the fabric of our reality. By understanding and harnessing the power of these mental constructs, we unlock the limitless potential to create the life of our dreams. As we cultivate a mindset of positivity, empowerment, and abundance, we pave the way for miracles to unfold, and blessings to abound. So, dare to dream boldly, believe fiercely, and watch as the universe conspires to manifest your deepest desires into reality.

Harnessing Visualization and Affirmations in Manifestation

In the intricate dance of manifestation, visualization and affirmations emerge as potent tools, capable of transforming dreams into reality and aspirations into actuality. These practices, rooted in the power of the mind, serve as gateways to the subconscious, allowing us to imprint our desires with clarity and conviction. As we delve into their role in the manifestation process, we embark on a journey of self-discovery and empowerment, unlocking the boundless potential that resides within.

Visualization, often described as the art of mentally creating vivid images of our desired outcomes, serves as a powerful catalyst in the manifestation process. By engaging our imagination and sensory faculties, we bring our aspirations to life, imbuing them with emotion, detail, and vibrancy. Through visualization, we not only clarify our intentions but also evoke the feelings associated with the realization of our dreams, signaling to the universe our readiness to receive.

When we visualize our desired outcomes with clarity and conviction, we activate the creative forces of the subconscious mind. The subconscious, unable to distinguish between reality and imagination, interprets our visualizations as instructions to manifest our desires into tangible form. As we consistently reinforce these mental images with positive emotions and belief, we establish a powerful resonance with our intentions, setting in motion the manifestation process.

Affirmations, or positive statements of intent, serve as potent tools for reprogramming the subconscious mind and aligning our thoughts with our desires. By repeating affirmations regularly, we reinforce empowering beliefs and intentions, replacing limiting narratives with new, empowering ones. Affirmations act as seeds planted in the fertile soil of the subconscious, germinating into manifestations of abundance, success, and fulfilment.

Affirmations operate on the principle of autosuggestion, harnessing the power of repetition and belief to rewire the neural pathways of the brain. When we affirm our desires with conviction and sincerity, we create new thought patterns that align with our aspirations, thereby magnetizing corresponding experiences into our lives. Affirmations serve as affirmations of our inherent worthiness, deservingness, and capability, affirming our ability to manifest our deepest desires.

When used in tandem, visualization and affirmations synergize to amplify the manifestation process, reinforcing each other's effectiveness and potency. Visualization provides the imagery and emotion, while affirmations provide the language and intention, creating a harmonious alignment between mind, body, and spirit. Together, these practices create a powerful resonance that catalyzes the manifestation of our desires with greater speed and precision.

As we embrace the transformative potential of visualization and affirmations, we step into our power as conscious creators of our reality. Through the practice of visualization, we paint the canvas of our imagination with the colors of our dreams, bringing them to life with vivid detail and emotion. Through affirmations, we infuse our thoughts with the energy of intention, planting seeds of empowerment and abundance in the fertile soil of the subconscious mind.

So, dare to visualize boldly, affirm fiercely, and watch as the universe conspires to manifest your deepest desires into reality. As you harness the power of visualization and affirmations, remember that the key lies not only in the practice itself but in the unwavering belief in your inherent ability to manifest your dreams. With each visualization and affirmation, you affirm your divine birthright to live a life of joy, abundance, and fulfilment.

Chapter 2: Self-Discovery and Setting Intentions

This chapter, embarks on an illuminating exploration of the self, uncovering hidden truths, clarifying intentions, and setting the stage for profound manifestation.

Self-discovery is not merely a journey of introspection but a sacred quest to unearth the essence of our being. It is a journey that invites us to peel back the layers of conditioning, societal expectations, and past experiences to reveal the core of our authentic selves. Through self-reflection, mindfulness practices, and inner exploration, we embark on a journey of self-discovery that illuminates the path to our true desires.

Intentions serve as the guiding lights that illuminate our path towards manifestation. In this chapter, we explore the art of setting clear and powerful intentions that align with our deepest desires. By articulating our intentions with clarity and precision, we harness the creative forces of the universe and pave the way for their realization. Through journaling exercises, visualization techniques, and guided meditations, we delve into the process of intention-setting, empowering you to clarify your goals, values, and priorities.

Authenticity lies at the heart of manifestation, for it is only when we align with our true selves that we can fully unleash our manifesting power. In this chapter, we celebrate the beauty of authenticity and encourage you to embrace your unique essence. By honoring your values, passions, and innate talents, you create a fertile ground for manifestation to flourish. Through authenticity, you tap into an infinite reservoir of creativity, inspiration, and abundance, allowing your true desires to blossom into reality.

Self-awareness is the cornerstone of personal growth and manifestation. In this chapter, we invite you to cultivate a deep sense of self-awareness through mindfulness practices, reflection, and self-inquiry. By becoming aware of your thoughts, emotions, and behavioral patterns, you gain insight into the underlying beliefs and conditioning that may be shaping your reality. Through self-awareness, you empower yourself to consciously choose thoughts, beliefs, and actions that align with your desires, thereby facilitating the manifestation process.

As we journey through the realms of self-discovery and intention-setting, we lay the groundwork for profound transformation and manifestation. By gaining clarity about your desires, values, and priorities, you set the stage for the manifestation of your dreams. Through authenticity, self-awareness, and intentional living, you empower yourself to create a life that is in alignment with your true purpose and highest potential.

As you embark on the journey of self-discovery and intention-setting, remember that you hold within you the power to manifest your deepest desires. By clarifying your intentions, embracing authenticity, and cultivating self-awareness, you unleash your manifesting power and create a life that reflects your true essence. So, let us continue this journey together, as we explore the depths of our being and set our intentions with unwavering clarity and conviction. The manifestation blueprint awaits, and your destiny beckons.

Embracing the Mirror Within

In the cacophony of modern life, amidst the hustle and bustle of daily routines and external distractions, it's all too easy to lose sight of the most essential aspect of our existence: ourselves. Yet, beneath the layers of societal expectations, cultural conditioning, and external influences lies a vast reservoir of wisdom, insight, and potential waiting to be unearthed. This treasure trove of self-awareness serves as the cornerstone of personal growth, empowerment, and fulfilment, guiding us on a journey of self-discovery and transformation. In this article, we explore the profound importance of self-awareness, unveiling its myriad benefits and offering practical insights into cultivating this invaluable trait.

At its essence, self-awareness can be defined as the ability to observe, understand, and accept oneself—both the light and shadow aspects of our being—with clarity and objectivity. It involves tuning into our thoughts, emotions, beliefs, and behaviors, and recognizing how they shape our perceptions, decisions, and interactions with the world. Self-awareness enables us to see ourselves as we truly are, free from the distortions of ego, judgment, and societal conditioning.

The benefits of cultivating self-awareness are manifold, extending to every aspect of our lives—personal, professional, and spiritual. Here are just a few of the many ways in which self-awareness enriches our existence:

Improved Emotional Intelligence: Self-awareness enhances our ability to recognize and regulate our emotions, fostering greater emotional resilience, empathy, and interpersonal relationships.

Enhanced Decision-Making: By understanding our values, priorities, and motivations, we make more informed and intentional decisions aligned with our true desires and aspirations.

Heightened Self-Confidence: Self-awareness cultivates a deep sense of self-acceptance and self-esteem, enabling us to embrace our strengths, weaknesses, and unique qualities with confidence and grace.

Greater Resilience: When faced with challenges and setbacks, self-aware individuals are better equipped to navigate adversity with resilience and grace, learning and growing from their experiences.

Empowered Relationships: By understanding our own needs, boundaries, and communication styles, we foster healthier, more authentic connections with others based on mutual respect, understanding, and compassion.

Personal Growth and Fulfilment: Self-awareness serves as the catalyst for personal growth and fulfilment, empowering us to live with purpose, passion, and authenticity.

While the benefits of self-awareness are undeniable, cultivating this trait requires dedication, practice, and patience. Here are some practical strategies to enhance self-awareness in your daily life:

Mindfulness Meditation: Engage in regular mindfulness meditation practices to cultivate present-moment awareness and observe your thoughts and emotions with curiosity and non-judgment.

Journaling: Set aside time each day to journal your thoughts, feelings, and experiences, allowing you to gain insights into your patterns, beliefs, and behaviors.

Self-Reflection: Carve out moments of solitude and silence to reflect on your values, goals, and aspirations, and contemplate how they align with your current thoughts and actions.

Seek Feedback: Solicit feedback from trusted friends, mentors, or coaches to gain external perspectives on your strengths, weaknesses, and blind spots.

Embrace Vulnerability: Practice vulnerability by acknowledging and accepting your imperfections, fears, and insecurities, recognizing that they are integral parts of your humanity.

Emotional Awareness Exercises: Engage in exercises such as body scanning, emotion labeling, or breath awareness to develop greater emotional intelligence and regulate your responses to challenging situations.

In a world that often prizes external achievements and accolades above inner wisdom and self-awareness, it's essential to recognize the profound importance of cultivating this invaluable trait. By embracing self-awareness, we embark on a journey of self-discovery and transformation, unlocking the door to greater emotional intelligence, resilience, and fulfilment. So, let us embrace the mirror within, for therein lies the key to unlocking our true potential and living a life of authenticity, purpose, and joy.

Navigating the Path Within

In the hustle and bustle of modern life, it's all too easy to get caught up in the relentless pursuit of external achievements and obligations, often at the expense of our deepest desires and aspirations. Yet, beneath the surface of our busy lives lies a quiet reservoir of dreams, passions, and aspirations waiting to be acknowledged, nurtured, and brought into fruition. In this article, we embark on a journey of self-reflection and introspection, guiding readers to connect with their innermost desires and chart a course towards a life of purpose, passion, and fulfilment.

Reflection serves as the compass that guides us on our journey of self-discovery and personal growth. It provides us with the opportunity to pause, introspect, and connect with our innermost thoughts, feelings, and aspirations. By taking the time to reflect on our goals and desires, we gain clarity about what truly matters to us and uncover the steps needed to manifest our dreams into reality.

In a world filled with noise and distractions, creating space for reflection is essential. Find a quiet and comfortable space where you can relax and be alone with your thoughts. This could be a cozy corner in your home, a serene spot in nature, or simply a few moments of solitude before bed. Set aside dedicated time each day or week for reflection, making it a non-negotiable part of your routine.

Guided Reflection Exercises:

To help guide your reflection process, consider engaging in the following exercises:

> **Journaling:** Set aside time each day to journal about your goals, desires, and aspirations. Write freely and without judgment, allowing your thoughts and feelings to flow onto the page. Explore questions such as: What are my most deeply held desires? What brings me joy and fulfilment? What are the obstacles that stand in the way of my goals?

> **Visualization:** Close your eyes and visualize yourself living your ideal life. Imagine every detail with vivid clarity—the sights, sounds, and sensations of your desired reality. Allow yourself to experience the emotions associated with achieving your goals, whether it's joy, excitement, or gratitude.

> **Mindfulness Meditation:** Practice mindfulness meditation to cultivate present-moment awareness and observe your thoughts and emotions with curiosity and non-judgment. Pay attention to any recurring themes or patterns that arise during your meditation practice, as they may offer valuable insights into your goals and desires.

> **Goal-Setting:** Take the time to set clear, specific, and achievable goals based on your reflections. Break down your goals into smaller, actionable steps, and create a timeline for

their attainment. Write them down and revisit them regularly to track your progress and stay motivated.

As you engage in the reflection process, it's important to approach yourself with kindness, compassion, and self-acceptance. Remember that reflection is not about self-criticism or judgment but about gaining insight and understanding. Be gentle with yourself and honor your feelings, even if they may be uncomfortable or challenging.

Armed with insights gained from reflection, it's time to take inspired action towards your goals and desires. Start by identifying one small step you can take today to move closer to your dreams, whether it's researching a new career path, enrolling in a course, or reaching out to a mentor for guidance. Trust in the process of manifestation, knowing that each step you take brings you closer to the life you envision.

As you embark on the journey of reflection, may you find clarity, inspiration, and purpose in the depths of your soul. May you reconnect with your deepest desires and aspirations, and may you have the courage to pursue them with unwavering determination and passion. Remember that your dreams are valid, your goals are achievable, and your journey is uniquely yours to navigate. So, take the time to reflect, to listen to the whispers of your heart, and to chart a course towards a life of meaning, fulfilment, and joy.

Setting Sail Towards Success

In the vast ocean of life, setting sail without a clear destination is akin to navigating without a compass—a journey fraught with uncertainty and aimlessness. Yet, with clear intentions as our guiding stars, we chart a course towards our desired destination with confidence, purpose, and unwavering determination. In this article, we delve into the transformative process of setting clear and positive intentions, illuminating the path towards manifestation and personal growth.

Intentions are the seeds from which our reality blossoms—they are the thoughts, beliefs, and desires that shape our experiences and guide our actions. Unlike goals, which are often concrete and measurable, intentions are more about the essence of what we wish to create or manifest in our lives. They serve as the guiding principles that align our thoughts, emotions, and actions with our deepest desires, paving the way for their realization.

The Process of Setting Intentions:

Reflect on Your Desires: Begin by taking the time to reflect on what you truly desire in various aspects of your life—whether it's relationships, career, health, or personal growth. Tune into your heart and soul, and identify the hopes, dreams, and aspirations that resonate most deeply with your authentic self.

Clarify Your Intentions: Once you've identified your desires, distill them into clear and concise intentions that encapsulate the essence of what you wish to manifest. Be specific yet flexible, focusing on the feelings and qualities you wish to cultivate rather than rigid outcomes. For example, instead of saying, "I want to lose 10 pounds," you might set the intention, "I intend to cultivate vibrant health and vitality in my body."

State Them Affirmatively: Phrase your intentions in the present tense, as if they are already true and unfolding in your life. This helps to program your subconscious mind for success and reinforces your belief in their attainment. For example, instead of saying, "I will find my soulmate someday," you might affirm, "I am attracting deep and fulfilling love into my life now."

Visualize Your Intentions: Take time each day to visualize your intentions as if they are already manifesting in your life. Close your eyes and immerse yourself in the sights, sounds, and sensations of living your intentions, allowing yourself to feel the emotions associated with their fulfilment. Visualization helps to anchor your intentions in your subconscious mind and align your energy with their manifestation.

Release Attachments: While it's essential to set clear intentions, it's equally important to release attachments to specific outcomes and trust in the divine timing of the universe. Surrendering control and allowing room for miracles to unfold opens the door to unexpected opportunities and blessings beyond what you can imagine.

Positive intentions act as the catalysts for transformation, infusing our lives with optimism, purpose, and joy. When we set positive intentions, we shift our focus from lack and limitation to abundance and possibility, opening ourselves to receive the blessings and opportunities that align with our highest good. Positive intentions also serve as powerful affirmations of our worthiness and deservingness, reminding us that we are co-creators of our reality and deserving of all the blessings life has to offer.

In the process of setting intentions, alignment plays a crucial role. Alignment refers to the harmony between your intentions, beliefs, emotions, and actions. When your intentions are aligned with your core values, beliefs, and desires, you create a powerful resonance that accelerates their manifestation. Conversely, when there is discord between your intentions and your inner landscape, it creates resistance and impedes the manifestation process.

To ensure alignment, it's essential to examine your beliefs and emotions surrounding your intentions. Identify any limiting beliefs or doubts that may be holding you back and work on shifting them into more empowering perspectives. Cultivate a mindset of positivity, abundance, and possibility, anchoring your intentions in a foundation of unwavering faith and belief in their realization.

Gratitude serves as a potent catalyst for manifestation, amplifying the energy of your intentions and opening the floodgates of abundance. When you express gratitude for the blessings already present in your life, you create a vibrational frequency that attracts more blessings into your reality. Incorporate gratitude practices into your daily routine, such as keeping a gratitude journal or offering silent thanks before meals, to cultivate a mindset of abundance and appreciation.

By infusing your intentions with gratitude, you elevate their potency and invite the universe to conspire in your favor. Rather than focusing solely on what you lack or desire, shift your attention to the blessings already present in your life, trusting that more abundance is on its way.

While setting intentions is a powerful first step, it's essential to follow them up with inspired action. Inspired action refers to actions taken from a place of alignment, intuition, and inner guidance, rather than fear, doubt, or obligation. When you align your actions with your intentions and intuition, you create momentum and move closer to the realization of your goals.

Listen to your inner wisdom and intuition, and allow them to guide you towards the next steps on your journey. Trust that the universe will present opportunities and synchronicities aligned with your intentions, and be open to receiving them with grace and gratitude. Remember that manifestation is a co-creative process between you and the universe, and by taking inspired action, you play an active role in bringing your intentions to life.

As you delve deeper into the process of setting clear and positive intentions, may you awaken to the limitless potential within you and embrace the role of conscious creator in your life. Remember that intention-setting is not a one-time event but an ongoing practice of aligning your thoughts, beliefs, emotions, and actions with your deepest desires. With clarity, positivity, and inspired action, you unlock the door to infinite possibilities and invite the manifestation of your wildest dreams into reality. So, set your intentions with intention, align your energy with your desires, and watch as the universe conspires to bring your visions to fruition.

Chapter 3: Building a Strong Foundation

In this chapter, we delve into the essential elements that form the bedrock of successful manifestation, guiding the reader on a path of self-awareness, belief transformation, and confidence cultivation.

Just as a sturdy foundation is essential for the stability and longevity of a building, so too is a strong foundation crucial for the manifestation of our desires. Without a solid footing rooted in clarity, belief, and self-confidence, our dreams risk being swept away by the winds of doubt and uncertainty. In this chapter, we explore the foundational principles that underpin successful manifestation, equipping you with the tools and insights needed to nurture the seeds of your desires into full bloom.

At the heart of manifestation lies our belief systems—the deeply ingrained beliefs and perceptions that shape our reality and influence our ability to manifest our desires. In this section, we delve into the role of belief systems in the manifestation process, exploring how our beliefs can either empower or hinder our ability to attract abundance, success, and fulfilment into our lives. Through introspection and inquiry, we uncover the beliefs that may be holding us back and learn how to cultivate beliefs that support our highest aspirations.

Self-limiting beliefs are the silent saboteurs that lurk in the shadows of our subconscious, whispering tales of doubt, unworthiness, and scarcity. In this segment, we shine a light on these limiting beliefs, identifying common narratives that may be sabotaging our manifestation efforts. Through practical exercises and strategies, we learn how to challenge and overcome these beliefs, replacing them with empowering narratives that align with our true potential and aspirations.

Confidence is the fuel that propels us forward on the journey of manifestation, empowering us to take bold actions and embrace the unknown with courage and conviction. In this chapter, we explore the practices and techniques for cultivating self-confidence, from visualization and positive self-talk to goal-setting and resilience-building. Through consistent practice and self-compassion, we learn to stand tall in our worthiness and capability, ready to manifest our deepest desires with unwavering confidence.

Alignment and resilience serve as pillars of strength on the path to manifestation, guiding us through the ebbs and flows of the journey. In this final section, we delve into the importance of aligning our thoughts, emotions, and actions with our desired outcomes, and we explore the resilience needed to navigate challenges and setbacks along the way. Through alignment and resilience, we forge ahead with clarity, purpose, and unwavering determination, knowing that we are capable of overcoming any obstacle in pursuit of our dreams.

Exploring the Impact of Belief Systems on Manifestation

Our beliefs serve as the lenses through which we perceive the world, shaping our reality and influencing our ability to manifest our desires. From childhood experiences to societal conditioning, our belief systems are deeply ingrained and often operate at a subconscious level, guiding our thoughts, emotions, and actions. In the realm of manifestation, our beliefs play a pivotal role in determining the outcomes we attract into our lives, creating either pathways to success or barriers to fulfilment.

At the core of manifestation lies the principle that like attracts like— that our thoughts, beliefs, and emotions emit energetic frequencies that resonate with similar frequencies in the universe, thereby drawing corresponding experiences into our reality. This principle underscores the significance of our belief systems in shaping our manifestations, as our beliefs act as magnets that attract experiences and opportunities aligned with their vibrational frequency.

One of the key concepts in understanding the role of belief systems in manifestation is the notion of the "belief-achievement gap." This term refers to the disparity between what we consciously desire to achieve and what we subconsciously believe we are capable of achieving. In other words, our beliefs about ourselves, our worthiness, and our capabilities may not always align with our conscious desires, creating a disconnect that hinders our manifestation efforts.

Limiting beliefs are the invisible barriers that stand between us and our dreams, whispering tales of doubt, unworthiness, and scarcity. These beliefs often stem from past experiences, societal conditioning, or fear-based narratives passed down through generations. For example, beliefs such as "I'm not good enough," "Success is reserved for others," or "I don't deserve happiness" can create self-imposed limitations that sabotage our ability to manifest our desires.

Yet, while limiting beliefs may hinder our manifestation efforts, they are not immutable truths set in stone. Through awareness, introspection, and intentional effort, we have the power to challenge and transform these beliefs, replacing them with empowering narratives that support our highest aspirations. By examining the origins of our beliefs and questioning their validity, we can begin to dismantle the barriers they create and open ourselves to new possibilities.

Empowering beliefs are the antidote to limiting beliefs, serving as catalysts for manifestation and success. These beliefs affirm our worthiness, capability, and deservingness of abundance, happiness, and fulfilment. Examples of empowering beliefs include:

> *"I am worthy of success and abundance in all areas of my life."*

> *"I am capable of achieving my dreams and creating the life I desire."*

> *"The universe is conspiring in my favor, and everything is unfolding for my highest good."*

> *"I trust in the divine timing of the universe and know that everything is happening as it should."*

By consciously adopting empowering beliefs and reinforcing them through affirmations, visualization, and positive self-talk, we reprogram our subconscious mind for success and create a fertile ground for manifestation to flourish. As we align our beliefs with our conscious desires, we bridge the gap between intention and manifestation, paving the way for the realization of our deepest desires.

Our belief systems play a profound role in shaping our perceptions of reality and influencing our ability to manifest our desires. By recognizing the impact of limiting beliefs and embracing empowering narratives, we empower ourselves to transcend self-imposed limitations and create a life aligned with our highest aspirations. As we examine and potentially shift our belief systems, we unlock the door to infinite possibilities and invite the manifestation of our wildest dreams into reality.

Navigating Beyond Self-Limiting Beliefs: A Path to Liberation

In the intricate tapestry of our minds, self-limiting beliefs lurk like shadows, casting doubt and uncertainty on our journey of manifestation. These beliefs, often ingrained from early experiences or societal conditioning, serve as silent saboteurs, whispering tales of unworthiness, scarcity, and failure. Yet, while self-limiting beliefs may cloak our potential in darkness, they are not insurmountable obstacles. In this article, we delve into the depths of self-limiting beliefs, exploring their impact on manifestation and offering strategies for overcoming them to unlock the boundless potential within.

Self-limiting beliefs take on myriad forms, yet common themes often revolve around feelings of unworthiness, scarcity, or failure. Beliefs such as "I'm not good enough," "There's never enough to go around," or "I'm destined to fail" can create invisible barriers that sabotage our manifestation efforts. These beliefs operate at a subconscious level, influencing our thoughts, emotions, and actions, and creating a self-fulfilling prophecy that reinforces their validity.

To overcome self-limiting beliefs, the first step is to shine a light on the shadows—to identify and acknowledge the beliefs that are holding us back from realizing our full potential. This process requires self-awareness and introspection, as we examine the narratives that shape our perceptions of ourselves and the world around us. By shining the light of awareness on our self-limiting beliefs, we take the first crucial step towards liberation from their grip.

Once we've identified our self-limiting beliefs, the next step is to challenge and reframe them through cognitive restructuring. This involves examining the evidence that supports or contradicts our beliefs and replacing distorted or irrational thoughts with more balanced and empowering perspectives. For example, if we hold a belief of unworthiness, we can gather evidence of our accomplishments, strengths, and positive qualities to challenge the validity of this belief. Through cognitive reframing, we gradually weaken the grip of self-limiting beliefs and create space for new, empowering narratives to take root.

Affirmations serve as powerful tools for reprogramming the subconscious mind and reinforcing empowering beliefs. By crafting positive affirmations that counteract our self-limiting beliefs and repeating them regularly with conviction and belief, we plant seeds of possibility in the fertile soil of our subconscious. Affirmations such as "I am worthy of success and abundance," "I attract opportunities for growth and prosperity," or "I am capable of achieving my dreams" can gradually reshape our beliefs and perceptions, paving the way for manifestation and transformation.

In addition to cognitive reframing and affirmation practices, cultivating a growth mindset is essential for overcoming self-limiting beliefs and embracing the possibility of success. A growth mindset is characterized by a belief in one's ability to learn, grow, and adapt in the face of challenges. By reframing failures and setbacks as opportunities for growth and learning, we shift our perspective from one of limitation to one of possibility. With a growth mindset, we approach life with curiosity, resilience, and optimism, knowing that our potential is limitless and that success is not defined by our past experiences or perceived limitations.

Self-limiting beliefs are formidable foes on the path to manifestation, yet they are not invincible adversaries. Through awareness, cognitive reframing, affirmation practices, and cultivating a growth mindset, we can overcome the grip of self-limiting beliefs and unlock the door to infinite possibilities. As we challenge the narratives that confine us and embrace the possibility of success, we step into our power as conscious creators of our reality, ready to manifest our deepest desires and live a life of purpose, abundance, and fulfilment.

Nurturing the Seeds of Self-Confidence

Self-confidence is the cornerstone of personal empowerment—a deep reservoir of inner strength and resilience that propels us forward on the path to manifesting our dreams. Yet, for many of us, cultivating self-confidence is a journey riddled with challenges and self-doubt. In this article, we explore practical techniques and exercises for building self-confidence, nurturing a mindset of self-compassion, and celebrating the inherent worthiness and capability within each of us.

One powerful practice for cultivating self-confidence is visualization—a technique that harnesses the power of the imagination to create a mental blueprint of success. By vividly imagining ourselves achieving our goals and embodying the qualities of confidence, competence, and self-assurance, we prime our subconscious mind for success. Visualization allows us to step into the role of our most confident selves, rehearsing success in our minds before it manifests in reality. Through regular visualization exercises, we cultivate a deep sense of belief in our abilities and strengthen our inner conviction.

Positive self-talk is another indispensable tool for building self-confidence, serving as the soundtrack of empowerment that plays in the background of our minds. By replacing self-critical thoughts with affirming and supportive messages, we shift our internal dialogue from one of self-doubt to one of self-empowerment. Affirmations such as "I am capable and competent," "I believe in my abilities," and "I deserve success" serve as powerful antidotes to self-limiting beliefs and bolster our sense of self-worth. Through consistent practice, positive self-talk becomes second nature, reinforcing our confidence and resilience in the face of challenges.

Goal-setting is a fundamental practice for building self-confidence, providing a roadmap for growth and achievement. By setting clear, achievable goals that stretch our comfort zones and challenge us to grow, we create opportunities for success and progress. Break down larger goals into smaller, actionable steps, and celebrate each milestone along the way. Each accomplishment serves as evidence of our capabilities and reinforces our belief in our ability to succeed. Through the pursuit of meaningful goals, we cultivate a sense of purpose and direction, strengthening our confidence and resilience in the process.

In the journey of building self-confidence, self-compassion is a guiding light that illuminates our path with warmth and acceptance. Embracing imperfection and treating ourselves with kindness and understanding allows us to navigate setbacks and failures with grace and resilience. Rather than berating ourselves for mistakes or shortcomings, we recognize them as opportunities for growth and learning. Self-compassion fosters a sense of inner peace and acceptance, freeing us from the burden of perfectionism and allowing us to embrace our authentic selves fully.

Celebrating our achievements, no matter how small, is essential for nurturing self-confidence and reinforcing our sense of worthiness and capability. Take the time to acknowledge and celebrate your successes, however modest they may seem. Whether it's completing a task, overcoming a fear, or stepping outside your comfort zone, each achievement is a testament to your courage and resilience. By acknowledging your accomplishments and celebrating your progress, you affirm your inherent worthiness and capability, fueling your self-confidence and empowering you to reach even greater heights.

Building self-confidence is a journey of self-discovery and empowerment—a journey that begins with belief in oneself and culminates in the realization of one's fullest potential. Through practices such as visualization, positive self-talk, goal-setting, self-compassion, and celebration of achievements, we nurture the seeds of self-confidence within us, allowing them to blossom into radiant expressions of empowerment and resilience. As we cultivate self-confidence, we step into our power as conscious creators of our reality, ready to manifest our deepest desires and live a life of purpose, passion, and fulfilment.

Unveiling the Power of Alignment

In the grand symphony of existence, alignment serves as the conductor, orchestrating the harmonious interplay of our beliefs, thoughts, emotions, and actions towards the manifestation of our deepest desires. Alignment is the sacred dance between our internal world—the realm of our thoughts, beliefs, and emotions—and our external reality—the canvas upon which our dreams take shape. In this article, we delve into the transformative power of alignment, exploring how coherence between our inner and outer worlds fosters a strong foundation for manifestation and paves the way for the realization of our highest aspirations.

At its essence, alignment is the art of bringing our inner landscape into resonance with our desired outcomes, aligning our beliefs, thoughts, emotions, and actions towards a common purpose. When our internal world is in harmony with our external reality, we create a powerful energetic vortex that magnetizes our desires towards us with effortless ease. Alignment is not merely about wishful thinking or positive affirmations; it is about embodying the energy of our desires at every level of our being and allowing them to manifest in our external reality.

Central to the power of alignment is the principle of coherence—the seamless integration and synchronization of our internal and external worlds. When our beliefs, thoughts, emotions, and actions are in alignment with our desired outcomes, we create a state of energetic coherence that amplifies the manifestation process. Like tuning forks vibrating in harmony, our internal and external worlds resonate with the frequency of our desires, attracting corresponding experiences and opportunities into our reality.

Maintaining alignment requires diligent awareness and conscious intentionality, as we navigate the ebb and flow of life's ever-changing currents. It is a continuous practice of tuning into our inner guidance system, listening to the whispers of our intuition, and course-correcting as needed to stay on the path of alignment. When we stray from alignment, we may experience resistance, struggle, or stagnation—signs that we are out of sync with our true desires and need to realign our thoughts, beliefs, and actions accordingly.

Alignment fosters a strong foundation for manifestation by creating a fertile ground for our desires to take root and flourish. When our internal landscape is free from the weeds of doubt, fear, and resistance, we allow the seeds of our desires to germinate and grow with vitality and abundance. Alignment infuses our manifestations with clarity, purpose, and intentionality, guiding them towards fruition with unwavering precision and grace.

To cultivate alignment, it is essential to cultivate practices that foster coherence between our inner and outer worlds. Mindfulness meditation, visualization, and journaling are powerful tools for aligning our thoughts, beliefs, and emotions with our desired outcomes. By engaging in these practices regularly, we train our minds to focus on what we want rather than what we fear, thereby shifting our energetic vibration towards manifestation.

Alignment also involves aligning our actions with our intentions, taking inspired action towards our goals and desires. When our thoughts, beliefs, and emotions are in alignment with our desired outcomes, our actions become infused with purpose and intentionality, propelling us towards our goals with clarity and determination. By aligning our beliefs, thoughts, emotions, and actions towards a common purpose, we create a synergistic flow of energy that accelerates the manifestation process and brings our desires into reality with effortless ease.

In essence, alignment is the sacred dance of creation—the harmonious integration of our inner and outer worlds towards the manifestation of our deepest desires. When we align our beliefs, thoughts, emotions, and actions with our desired outcomes, we create a powerful energetic vortex that magnetizes our dreams towards us with unstoppable force. Alignment fosters a strong foundation for manifestation, infusing our desires with clarity, purpose, and intentionality, and guiding them towards fruition with unwavering precision and grace. As we align our inner and outer worlds, we step into our power as conscious creators of our reality, ready to manifest our wildest dreams and live a life of purpose, passion, and fulfilment.

Cultivating Resilience and Persistence

In the labyrinth of life, the journey towards manifestation is often fraught with twists and turns, obstacles and setbacks. Yet, it is through the crucible of challenges that we forge the steel of resilience and the fire of persistence—qualities that propel us forward on the path towards our deepest desires. In this article, we explore the significance of resilience and persistence in overcoming obstacles and setbacks on the journey of manifestation, and we delve into strategies for cultivating these essential qualities to navigate the ebbs and flows of life with grace and determination.

Resilience is the unwavering strength that allows us to bounce back from adversity, to rise from the ashes of defeat, and to emerge stronger and more resilient than before. In the face of challenges and setbacks, resilience enables us to maintain our composure, to adapt to changing circumstances, and to persevere in the pursuit of our goals. It is the inner fortitude that sustains us through the storms of life, reminding us of our inherent capacity to overcome even the most daunting obstacles.

One key strategy for cultivating resilience is reframing setbacks as opportunities for growth and learning. Rather than viewing challenges as insurmountable obstacles, we can choose to see them as stepping stones on the path to our highest potential. By shifting our perspective and embracing a growth mindset, we transform setbacks into catalysts for transformation, extracting valuable lessons and insights from every experience. Through the lens of resilience, setbacks become not barriers to manifestation, but gateways to expansion and evolution.

Practicing self-compassion is another essential strategy for cultivating resilience in the face of adversity. Self-compassion involves treating ourselves with kindness, understanding, and acceptance, especially during times of struggle or difficulty. Rather than berating ourselves for perceived failures or shortcomings, we extend ourselves the same grace and compassion that we would offer to a dear friend in need. By cultivating self-compassion, we build a reservoir of inner strength and resilience that sustains us through life's inevitable challenges.

Maintaining a positive mindset despite obstacles is also crucial for fostering resilience and persistence on the journey of manifestation. A positive mindset allows us to see beyond the immediate challenges and setbacks, to envision a brighter future, and to remain steadfast in our pursuit of our goals. By focusing on what is possible rather than dwelling on what is lacking, we shift our energy towards manifestation and empowerment, harnessing the power of optimism and hope to propel us forward on our path.

Persistence is the unwavering commitment to our goals and desires, the steadfast determination to continue moving forward in the face of adversity. It is the refusal to be deterred by setbacks or obstacles, the resilience to persevere even when the road ahead seems long and arduous. In the journey of manifestation, persistence is the engine that drives us towards our dreams, the fuel that propels us forward through challenges and setbacks.

To cultivate persistence, it is essential to maintain a clear vision of our goals and desires, to keep our eyes firmly fixed on the prize even when the path ahead is obscured by clouds of doubt or uncertainty. Visualization and goal-setting are powerful tools for clarifying our intentions and maintaining focus on our desired outcomes, allowing us to navigate through challenges with clarity and determination. By holding onto our vision with unwavering faith and commitment, we infuse our journey with purpose and meaning, and we continue moving forward towards manifestation with courage and resilience.

Resilience and persistence are indispensable qualities on the journey of manifestation, serving as beacons of light that guide us through the darkest of times and propel us towards our brightest dreams. By cultivating resilience through reframing setbacks as opportunities for growth, practicing self-compassion, and maintaining a positive mindset despite obstacles, and by nurturing persistence through clear vision and unwavering commitment to our goals, we empower ourselves to overcome any challenge and to manifest our deepest desires with grace and determination. As we embrace the journey with resilience and persistence, we step into our power as conscious creators of our reality, ready to manifest a life of purpose, passion, and fulfilment.

Chapter 4: Visualization Techniques

This chapter delves into the transformative power of visualization techniques—a practice that harnesses the creative power of the mind to manifest our deepest desires into reality. Visualization is not merely about imagining a desired outcome; it is about stepping into the vibrant tapestry of our dreams, painting vivid scenes of success, abundance, and fulfilment that resonate with our deepest desires. Join us as we explore various visualization exercises and techniques, share real-life success stories that illustrate the potency of visualization, and offer practical tips for enhancing your visualization skills to bring your dreams to life.

Our journey begins with an exploration of the diverse array of visualization exercises and techniques at our disposal. From guided imagery to vision boards, mental rehearsal to sensory visualization, each technique offers a unique approach to activating the creative power of the mind and aligning our thoughts with our desired outcomes. Through practical guidance and step-by-step instructions, we invite you to embark on a journey of self-discovery and transformation as you explore the limitless possibilities of visualization.

As we immerse ourselves in the world of visualization, we are inspired by the real-life success stories of individuals who have manifested their dreams through the power of visualization. From achieving career milestones to finding love, overcoming health challenges to experiencing financial abundance, these stories serve as beacons of hope and inspiration, illustrating the transformative impact of visualization on every aspect of life. Join us as we journey alongside these visionaries and glean insights that illuminate the path towards our own manifestations.

To master the art of visualization, we must hone our skills and cultivate a mindset of mastery and refinement. In this section, we offer practical tips and strategies for enhancing your visualization skills, from creating an optimal environment for visualization to engaging the senses and cultivating emotional engagement. Whether you are a seasoned practitioner or new to the practice of visualization, these tips will empower you to deepen your practice, strengthen your connection to your desires, and unleash the full potential of your creative power.

Along the journey of visualization, we may encounter obstacles and challenges that test our resolve and commitment. In this section, we explore common challenges such as difficulty focusing, skepticism, or impatience, and offer strategies for overcoming them with resilience and grace. By navigating through these challenges with courage and perseverance, we emerge stronger and more resilient, ready to continue our journey towards manifestation with unwavering determination.

As we conclude our exploration of visualization techniques, we invite you to weave the practice of visualization into the fabric of your daily life. From morning rituals to visualization prompts, visualization tools to creative visualization, there are countless ways to infuse your daily routines with the magic of visualization. By integrating visualization into your daily life, you not only strengthen your manifestation practice but also cultivate a deeper sense of presence, purpose, and empowerment in every moment.

As we embark on this visual journey of transformation and manifestation, we invite you to open your mind and heart to the infinite possibilities that await. Through the practice of visualization, we awaken to the creative power within us, painting our dreams into reality one vibrant brushstroke at a time. Join us as we step boldly into the canvas of imagination and co-create a life filled with joy, abundance, and fulfilment.

Visualization Techniques

Visualization is a powerful tool that harnesses the creative power of the mind to manifest our deepest desires into reality. At its core, visualization involves mentally picturing specific outcomes, scenarios, or experiences with the intention of bringing them to fruition. Whether it's achieving career success, finding love, improving health, or experiencing financial abundance, visualization empowers us to paint the canvas of our dreams with vivid detail and clarity.

The importance of visualization in manifestation cannot be overstated. Our thoughts have a profound impact on our reality, shaping the energetic vibrations we emit and attracting corresponding experiences into our lives. Visualization acts as a bridge between our internal world—the realm of our thoughts, beliefs, and emotions—and our external reality, aligning our desires with the universal flow of energy and setting the stage for manifestation to unfold.

By engaging in visualization exercises, we activate the creative power of our subconscious mind, programming it with images of success, abundance, and fulfilment. These mental images serve as blueprints for the reality we wish to create, guiding our thoughts, emotions, and actions towards our desired outcomes. Through consistent practice, visualization strengthens our belief in the possibility of manifestation, amplifies our intentions, and accelerates the manifestation process.

Guided Imagery: Navigating the Landscape of the Mind

Guided imagery is a visualization technique that involves mentally picturing specific scenes, scenarios, or experiences with the guidance of a narrator or recorded script. It provides a structured framework for visualization, guiding participants through a series of imagery exercises designed to evoke specific emotions and sensations.

To practice guided imagery, find a quiet and comfortable space where you won't be disturbed. Close your eyes, take a few deep breaths, and relax your body and mind. Then, listen to a guided imagery recording or follow along with a scripted visualization exercise. As you listen, allow yourself to fully immerse in the imagery, engaging all of your senses to create a vivid and lifelike experience.

Guided imagery is particularly effective for deep relaxation, stress reduction, and accessing the subconscious mind. By engaging the imagination in a focused and intentional way, guided imagery bypasses the analytical mind and accesses the deeper layers of consciousness where true transformation occurs. Whether it's visualizing yourself achieving a specific goal, overcoming a challenge, or experiencing a sense of inner peace and tranquility, guided imagery can be a powerful tool for manifestation and personal growth.

Mental Rehearsal: Scripting Your Success

Mental rehearsal, also known as mental practice or visualization rehearsal, is a technique used to mentally rehearse desired outcomes or scenarios in order to improve performance and increase the likelihood of success. It involves vividly imagining yourself achieving a specific goal, overcoming a challenge, or mastering a skill with as much detail and clarity as possible.

To practice mental rehearsal, find a quiet and comfortable space where you can relax and focus your attention. Close your eyes and visualize yourself in the desired situation, engaging all of your senses to create a vivid and realistic experience. Imagine yourself performing the desired actions with confidence and precision, feeling the emotions associated with success, and experiencing the outcomes you wish to manifest.

Mental rehearsal is particularly effective for improving performance in sports, academics, and other areas where skill mastery is required. By mentally rehearsing success, you strengthen the neural pathways associated with the desired actions, increase your confidence and self-efficacy, and enhance your ability to perform at your best when it matters most. Whether you're preparing for a presentation, a job interview, or a competitive event, mental rehearsal can help you achieve your goals with greater ease and effectiveness.

Vision Boards: Crafting Your Vision of Success

Vision boards are visual representations of our goals, dreams, and desires, created by compiling images, words, and symbols that evoke the feelings and experiences we wish to manifest. They serve as powerful tools for clarifying our intentions, reinforcing our beliefs, and aligning our thoughts and emotions with our desired outcomes.

To create a vision board, gather magazines, newspapers, photographs, and other visual materials that resonate with your goals and aspirations. Then, select images, words, and symbols that capture the essence of what you wish to manifest in your life. Arrange these elements on a poster board, corkboard, or digital collage in a way that feels meaningful and inspiring to you.

Once your vision board is complete, place it in a prominent location where you will see it frequently—such as your bedroom, office, or meditation space. Spend time each day visualizing yourself living the experiences and achieving the goals depicted on your vision board, engaging all of your senses to make the images come alive in your mind.

Vision boards are powerful tools for manifestation because they tap into the visual-spatial processing centers of the brain, making our goals and desires more tangible and accessible. By surrounding ourselves with images of success, abundance, and fulfilment, we create a constant reminder of what we are working towards and cultivate a deep sense of belief in our ability to manifest our dreams.

Sensory Visualization: Engaging All Five Senses

Sensory visualization involves engaging all five senses—sight, hearing, touch, taste, and smell—during visualization exercises to enhance the depth and intensity of the experience. By incorporating sensory details into our visualizations, we make them more vivid, immersive, and emotionally resonant, amplifying their impact on the subconscious mind and accelerating the manifestation process.

To practice sensory visualization, begin by relaxing your body and mind in a quiet and comfortable space. Close your eyes and take a few deep breaths to center yourself. Then, imagine yourself in the desired situation or scenario, and consciously engage each of your senses to create a multi-dimensional experience.

For example, if you're visualizing yourself walking on a beach, imagine the warmth of the sun on your skin, the sound of waves crashing against the shore, the sensation of sand between your toes, the taste of salt in the air, and the scent of coconut sunscreen. By vividly imagining these sensory details, you immerse yourself in the experience and make it feel more real and tangible.

Sensory visualization is particularly effective for deepening emotional engagement, strengthening belief in the manifestation process, and accelerating the realization of desired outcomes. By engaging all of your senses, you create a holistic experience that resonates with every aspect of your being, aligning your thoughts, emotions, and actions with your desired reality.

In conclusion, visualization exercises and techniques offer powerful tools for manifestation and personal growth. Whether it's guided imagery, mental rehearsal, vision boards, or sensory visualization, each technique provides a unique approach to activating the creative power of the mind and aligning our thoughts with our desired outcomes. By incorporating these visualization practices into our daily lives, we empower ourselves to paint the canvas of our dreams with vivid detail and clarity, and manifest our deepest desires into reality with grace and ease.

Enhancing Visualization Skills

Visualization is a powerful tool for manifesting our deepest desires into reality, but like any skill, it requires practice and refinement to master. In this article, we will explore tips and techniques for enhancing your visualization skills, empowering you to paint the canvas of your dreams with vivid detail and clarity.

Creating the right environment is crucial for effective visualization. Find a quiet and comfortable space where you won't be disturbed, and ensure that the lighting is soft and soothing. Dim the lights or use candles to create a warm and inviting ambiance that promotes relaxation and focus. Consider incorporating elements of nature, such as plants or natural scents, to enhance the sense of tranquility and connection to the earth. Lastly, choose a comfortable seating position or lie down if preferred, allowing your body to fully relax and your mind to enter a state of receptivity.

To make your visualizations more vivid and immersive, engage all of your senses in the experience. As you visualize, imagine not only what you see but also what you hear, feel, smell, and taste. For example, if you're visualizing yourself on a beach, imagine the sound of waves crashing against the shore, the warmth of the sun on your skin, the sensation of sand between your toes, the scent of salt in the air, and the taste of a refreshing drink. By incorporating sensory details into your visualizations, you make them more lifelike and emotionally resonant, amplifying their impact on your subconscious mind and accelerating the manifestation process.

Consistency is key to mastering visualization. Set aside dedicated time each day to practice visualization, ideally in the morning or before bedtime when your mind is most receptive. Start with short sessions and gradually increase the duration as you become more comfortable with the practice. Consistent practice reinforces neural pathways associated with your desired outcomes, strengthening your belief in the manifestation process and deepening your connection to your goals. Treat visualization like any other skill or habit—commit to it wholeheartedly and watch as it transforms your reality from the inside out.

Emotions are the fuel that powers manifestation, so it's essential to tap into the emotions associated with your desired outcomes during visualization. As you visualize, allow yourself to feel the joy, excitement, and gratitude that come with achieving your goals. Imagine how it would feel to live your desired reality, and let those feelings wash over you like a warm embrace. The more emotionally engaged you are in your visualizations, the more potent they become, amplifying the manifestation process and bringing your dreams to life with greater ease and speed.

Finally, it's crucial to let go of attachment to specific outcomes during visualization and trust in the universe's timing and wisdom. Understand that the universe works in mysterious ways and may have plans for you that are even better than what you can imagine. Surrender to the flow of life, release any resistance or attachment, and trust that everything is unfolding exactly as it should. By letting go of the need to control or force outcomes, you open yourself up to infinite possibilities and allow miracles to unfold in divine timing.

Enhancing your visualization skills is a journey of self-discovery and empowerment, allowing you to paint the canvas of your dreams with vivid detail and clarity. By creating an optimal environment for visualization, engaging all of your senses, practicing consistency, tapping into your emotions, and letting go of attachment, you empower yourself to manifest your deepest desires with grace and ease. Trust in the power of visualization, and watch as your dreams blossom into reality before your very eyes.

Overcoming Common Challenges in Visualization

Visualization is a powerful tool for manifesting our dreams into reality, but like any practice, it comes with its own set of challenges. In this article, we'll explore some common obstacles individuals may encounter during visualization and offer practical strategies for overcoming them, while emphasizing the importance of resilience in persisting through setbacks on the journey to manifestation.

One of the most common challenges individuals face in visualization is difficulty focusing. In today's fast-paced world, our minds are often scattered and distracted, making it challenging to maintain concentration during visualization exercises. Additionally, skepticism can creep in, causing doubt or disbelief in the effectiveness of visualization as a manifestation tool. Impatience is another obstacle, as individuals may become frustrated if they don't see immediate results from their visualization practice.

To overcome difficulty focusing, it's essential to create a conducive environment for visualization. Find a quiet and comfortable space, free from distractions, where you can fully immerse yourself in the practice. Set aside dedicated time each day for visualization, and consider using tools such as guided meditation or soothing music to help quiet the mind and enhance concentration. Additionally, practicing mindfulness techniques, such as deep breathing or body scanning, can help anchor your awareness in the present moment and reduce mental chatter.

When faced with skepticism, it's important to remind yourself of the countless success stories and scientific evidence supporting the efficacy of visualization as a manifestation tool. Keep a journal to track your progress and document any positive changes or synchronicities that occur as a result of your visualization practice. Surround yourself with supportive mentors or communities who can offer encouragement and validation, and seek out inspiring resources, such as books or podcasts, that reaffirm your belief in the power of visualization.

Impatience can be a challenging obstacle to overcome, especially in a society that values instant gratification. Remember that manifestation is a process, and results may not manifest overnight. Trust in the divine timing of the universe and surrender to the flow of life, knowing that your desires are being orchestrated behind the scenes. Practice gratitude for what you already have and focus on the journey rather than solely fixating on the destination. Cultivate patience and perseverance, knowing that every visualization practice brings you one step closer to your goals.

In addition to specific strategies for overcoming challenges, cultivating resilience is essential for persisting through setbacks on the visualization journey. Resilience is the ability to bounce back from adversity, to adapt to change, and to persevere in the face of challenges. It requires inner strength, determination, and a willingness to embrace discomfort as part of the growth process.

To cultivate resilience, practice self-care and self-compassion, treating yourself with kindness and understanding during difficult times. Lean on your support network for guidance and encouragement, and seek out mentors or role models who exemplify resilience in the face of adversity. Embrace failure as an opportunity for growth and learning, reframing setbacks as stepping stones on the path to success. Cultivate a growth mindset, focusing on solutions rather than dwelling on problems, and celebrate your progress, however small.

Overcoming common challenges in visualization requires awareness, intentionality, and resilience. By identifying obstacles such as difficulty focusing, skepticism, and impatience, and implementing practical strategies for addressing them, individuals can unlock the full potential of visualization as a manifestation tool. Cultivating resilience is essential for persisting through setbacks and staying committed to the visualization journey, knowing that every challenge is an opportunity for growth and transformation on the path to manifesting our deepest desires.

Incorporating Visualization into Daily Life: Weaving Dreams into Reality

Visualization is a powerful practice that can transform our desires into tangible manifestations, but its impact is maximized when integrated seamlessly into our daily routines. In this article, we'll explore practical ways to incorporate visualization into your everyday life, from morning rituals to bedtime routines, empowering you to weave your dreams into reality with grace and intention.

The morning is a sacred time for setting intentions and aligning with the energy of the day ahead. Incorporating visualization into your morning routine can help you start your day on a positive note and set the tone for success. Consider beginning your day with a visualization meditation, where you take a few moments to quiet your mind, connect with your inner vision, and visualize yourself achieving your goals with clarity and confidence. Alternatively, you can set intentions for the day ahead by visualizing how you want to feel, what you want to accomplish, and the actions you will take to manifest your desires.

Throughout the day, it's easy to get caught up in the busyness of life and lose sight of our intentions. Visualization prompts serve as gentle reminders to engage in brief visualization exercises, helping us stay aligned with our goals and desires amidst the chaos of daily life. Consider placing visual reminders, such as sticky notes or inspirational quotes, in strategic locations where you will see them throughout the day—on your desk, bathroom mirror, or refrigerator door. Use these prompts as cues to pause, take a deep breath, and visualize yourself moving closer to your goals, whether it's during a coffee break, commute, or moments of downtime.

In today's digital age, there is no shortage of tools and resources to support your visualization practice. Smartphone apps, guided meditation recordings, and online platforms offer convenient ways to access guided visualization exercises and immersive experiences that deepen your connection to your desires. Explore different visualization apps that align with your preferences and goals, whether you prefer guided meditations, visualization prompts, or customizable features. Experiment with different tools and find what resonates with you, incorporating them into your daily routine to support your visualization practice and amplify its effectiveness.

Visualization is not just about picturing your desired outcomes; it's about infusing your imagination with possibility and unleashing your creative potential. Creative visualization encourages you to experiment with different techniques, settings, and scenarios, allowing your imagination to roam freely and explore the endless possibilities that await. Consider incorporating elements of play, curiosity, and spontaneity into your visualization practice, whether it's visualizing yourself achieving success in a fantastical setting, interacting with your future self, or embodying the qualities of your ideal self. By infusing creativity into your visualization practice, you expand your capacity to manifest your desires and invite new possibilities into your life.

Incorporating visualization into your daily life is a powerful way to align with your desires, cultivate a positive mindset, and manifest your dreams with intention and purpose. Whether it's through morning rituals, visualization prompts, visualization tools, or creative visualization, find ways to weave visualization into the fabric of your daily routine, empowering yourself to live a life filled with joy, abundance, and fulfilment. As you infuse your everyday moments with the energy of your dreams, watch as your reality transforms before your very eyes, guided by the power of your imagination and the intention of your heart.

Chapter 5: The Power of Affirmations

In this chapter we dive into the transformative world of affirmations—a potent tool for harnessing the power of the mind to manifest our deepest desires. In this chapter, we'll explore the profound impact of affirmations on shifting beliefs, cultivating positivity, and aligning with the abundant possibilities that surround us.

Affirmations are more than just words; they are seeds of empowerment planted in the fertile soil of our subconscious minds. At their core, affirmations are positive statements or declarations that we repeat to ourselves with the intention of reprogramming our beliefs and manifesting our desires. Whether it's affirming our worthiness, abundance, or potential, affirmations have the power to transform our thoughts, emotions, and actions, paving the way for a life filled with joy, abundance, and fulfilment.

The purpose of affirmations is to shift limiting beliefs that hold us back from realizing our full potential. Throughout our lives, we absorb countless messages from society, family, and culture that shape our beliefs about ourselves and the world around us. These beliefs, whether positive or negative, influence every aspect of our lives, from our relationships to our career to our health. Affirmations act as a catalyst for change, challenging outdated beliefs and replacing them with new, empowering ones that align with our desires and aspirations.

Creating effective affirmations is both an art and a science. It requires clarity, positivity, and intentionality to ensure that our affirmations resonate with our subconscious minds and evoke the desired outcomes. In this chapter, we'll explore practical tips and strategies for crafting affirmations that pack a punch, from choosing empowering language to focusing on what we want (rather than what we don't want) to affirming our worthiness and deservingness.

Using affirmations daily is the key to unlocking their full potential. In this chapter, we'll explore different methods for incorporating affirmations into our daily routines, from morning rituals to affirmation journaling to digital reminders. By integrating affirmations seamlessly into our everyday lives, we make them a natural and effortless part of our existence, reinforcing positive beliefs and manifesting our desires with ease and grace.

No journey is without its challenges, and the path of affirmation is no exception. In this chapter, we'll explore common obstacles individuals may encounter when using affirmations, such as resistance, doubt, or lack of consistency, and offer practical strategies for overcoming them. By cultivating resilience and staying committed to our practice, we empower ourselves to overcome any challenge that arises and continue on the path to manifestation.

As we deepen our understanding of affirmations, we'll explore advanced techniques for enhancing their effectiveness, such as scripting, mirror work, and incorporating gratitude. These techniques offer new avenues for exploration and growth, empowering us to unlock new levels of manifestation and create the life of our dreams.

As we embark on this journey into the power of affirmations, I invite you to open your mind and heart to the infinite possibilities that await. Together, we'll explore the transformative potential of affirmations and unleash the magic within, one positive thought at a time. Get ready to witness the profound impact of affirmations on your life and step boldly into a future filled with joy, abundance, and fulfilment.

Affirmations and Their Purpose

Affirmations are more than mere words; they are potent tools for harnessing the power of the mind to shape our reality and manifest our deepest desires. At their essence, affirmations are positive statements or declarations that we repeat to ourselves with the intention of reprogramming our subconscious minds and aligning with our desired outcomes. These affirmations act as seeds planted in the fertile soil of our subconscious, nurturing the beliefs and thoughts that shape our perception of ourselves and the world around us.

The purpose of affirmations extends far beyond the realm of positive thinking; they serve as catalysts for profound transformation on both an internal and external level. One of the primary roles of affirmations is to shift limiting beliefs that hold us back from realizing our full potential. Throughout our lives, we internalize beliefs about ourselves and our capabilities, often based on past experiences or societal conditioning. These beliefs can act as invisible barriers, constraining our actions and limiting our possibilities. Affirmations challenge these limiting beliefs, replacing them with new, empowering ones that support our growth and success.

In addition to shifting limiting beliefs, affirmations play a crucial role in cultivating a positive mindset. Our thoughts have a powerful influence on our emotions, behaviors, and ultimately, our outcomes. By consistently affirming positive statements about ourselves and our lives, we train our minds to focus on the good, to see opportunities where others see obstacles, and to approach challenges with confidence and optimism. This positive mindset creates a ripple effect, attracting more positivity and abundance into our lives and propelling us toward our goals with greater ease and grace.

Furthermore, affirmations are instrumental in aligning with the energy of abundance and success. The universe operates on the principle of like attracts like; the thoughts and beliefs we hold emit a vibrational frequency that draws corresponding experiences into our reality. When we affirm statements of abundance, prosperity, and success, we align our energy with these desired outcomes, signaling to the universe that we are ready to receive. This alignment opens the floodgates of possibility, ushering in synchronicities, opportunities, and blessings that support our journey toward our goals.

The underlying principles of affirmations lay the foundation for their effectiveness as manifestation tools. At the core of affirmations lies the power of intention—the deliberate and conscious focus of our thoughts and desires toward a specific outcome. Intention infuses our affirmations with purpose and direction, guiding the energy of our thoughts toward the manifestation of our desires. Repetition is another key principle of affirmations, as it reinforces new beliefs and patterns in the subconscious mind. By repeating affirmations consistently, we strengthen neural pathways associated with our desired outcomes, making them more accessible and achievable. Finally, belief is the driving force behind affirmations; without belief in the power of our affirmations and the possibility of our desires, their effectiveness is diminished. Belief fuels our intentions, amplifying their impact and magnetizing our desires toward us with greater force.

Affirmations are powerful tools for transformation, capable of reshaping our beliefs, thoughts, and reality. By understanding the purpose of affirmations and embracing their underlying principles, we unlock the potential to manifest our deepest desires and create a life filled with joy, abundance, and fulfilment. As we harness the power of affirmations to align with our truest desires, we awaken to the infinite possibilities that await us and step boldly into a future of unlimited potential.

Effective Affirmations for Manifestation Success

Effective affirmations are like seeds planted in the fertile soil of our subconscious minds, nurturing beliefs and thoughts that shape our reality. Crafting affirmations that resonate with our goals and desires requires a thoughtful approach, understanding the key components that make them impactful and aligning them with our deepest aspirations. In this article, we'll explore practical guidance on creating effective affirmations that inspire and empower you to manifest the life of your dreams.

Understanding the components of effective affirmations is crucial for crafting statements that resonate deeply with your subconscious mind and evoke the desired outcomes. Clarity is essential, ensuring that your affirmations are specific and focused on a clear goal or intention. Positivity is another key component, as affirmations should be framed in a positive light, focusing on what you want to attract into your life rather than what you want to avoid. Using present tense language is also important, as it signals to your subconscious mind that your desired outcome is already happening in the present moment. Lastly, personalization adds depth and authenticity to your affirmations, making them more meaningful and relevant to your unique desires and experiences.

To craft affirmations that resonate with your goals and desires, consider using empowering language that evokes feelings of confidence, empowerment, and possibility. Choose words that resonate with you on a deep level and align with the energy of your desires. For example, instead of saying "I will try to be successful," say "I am successful in all areas of my life." This shift in language reinforces the belief that success is not only possible but inevitable.

Focus on what you want, rather than what you don't want, when crafting affirmations. The subconscious mind does not recognize negations, so affirmations framed in negative terms may inadvertently reinforce the very thing you're trying to avoid. Instead, focus on the positive outcome you desire and affirm it with conviction. For example, instead of saying "I don't want to be stressed," say "I am calm and at peace in every situation."

Affirm your worthiness and deservingness in your affirmations, recognizing that you are inherently worthy of love, abundance, and success. By affirming your worthiness, you remove any subconscious barriers or self-limiting beliefs that may be blocking your path to manifestation. Embrace the belief that you are deserving of all the blessings life has to offer, and watch as your reality begins to reflect this inner truth.

To inspire and spark your creativity, here are examples of effective affirmations for various areas of life:

Health:

> "I am vibrant and full of energy, radiating health and vitality."

> "Every cell in my body is thriving with optimal health and well-being."

Relationships:

> "I attract loving and supportive relationships into my life effortlessly."

> "I am surrounded by positive and uplifting people who uplift and inspire me."

Career:

> "I am highly skilled and competent in my work, achieving success with ease."

> "Opportunities for advancement and growth come to me effortlessly."

Abundance:

> "I am a magnet for abundance, attracting wealth and prosperity into my life."

> "The universe is conspiring in my favor, showering me with abundance in all forms."

As you craft your affirmations, remember to infuse them with your unique voice and intentions, making them a powerful reflection of your deepest desires and aspirations. By aligning your affirmations with the key components of clarity, positivity, present tense, and personalization, you set the stage for profound transformation and manifestation in every area of your life.

Daily Affirmations: Your Key to Consistent Manifestation Success

In the journey of manifestation, consistency is key. It's not just about setting intentions or crafting affirmations; it's about integrating these practices into our daily lives to create lasting change. In this article, we'll explore various methods for incorporating affirmations into your daily routine, offering guidance on how to make them a natural and effortless part of your everyday life.

Incorporating affirmations into your daily routine can take many forms, depending on your preferences and lifestyle. One method is to incorporate them into your morning rituals. Begin your day with a few moments of quiet reflection, where you repeat your affirmations aloud or silently, setting the tone for a positive and productive day ahead. You can also create an affirmation journal, where you write down your affirmations each morning or evening, reinforcing them through the act of writing and reflection. For those who prefer digital tools, setting reminders on your phone or computer can be an effective way to prompt yourself to practice affirmations throughout the day.

Integrating affirmations seamlessly into your existing routines and habits is essential for ensuring their effectiveness. Rather than treating affirmations as a separate practice, weave them into activities you already do regularly. For example, repeat your affirmations while brushing your teeth, taking a shower, or commuting to work. By associating affirmations with activities you already do without much thought, you make them a natural and effortless part of your daily life. Another strategy is to create visual reminders, such as sticky notes or affirmations cards, and place them in strategic locations where you will see them throughout the day, such as your desk, bathroom mirror, or refrigerator door.

Consistency and repetition are the cornerstones of effective affirmation practice. Just as a muscle grows stronger with regular exercise, our minds are strengthened through consistent repetition of positive thoughts and beliefs. Make a commitment to practice affirmations regularly, whether it's daily, multiple times a day, or whenever you feel the need for a mental boost. The more you repeat your affirmations, the more deeply they become ingrained in your subconscious mind, reinforcing positive beliefs and paving the way for manifestation. Remember that the power of affirmations lies not only in the words themselves but in the energy and intention behind them. Approach your affirmation practice with sincerity and conviction, trusting in the process and allowing the transformative power of consistency to work its magic.

Incorporating affirmations into your daily life is a powerful way to align with your desires, cultivate a positive mindset, and manifest your dreams with intention and purpose. By exploring different methods for integrating affirmations into your routine, making them a natural and effortless habit, and committing to consistency and repetition, you empower yourself to create lasting change and transform your reality from the inside out. As you embrace the power of daily affirmation practice, watch as your beliefs shift, your mindset expands, and your dreams begin to manifest with ease and grace.

Overcoming Affirmation Hurdles

Embarking on the journey of using affirmations to manifest your dreams is an empowering endeavor, but like any path to transformation, it comes with its fair share of challenges. Understanding and overcoming these hurdles is essential for unlocking the full potential of affirmations and achieving your desired outcomes. In this article, we'll explore some common challenges individuals may face when using affirmations and offer practical strategies for overcoming them with resilience, persistence, and patience.

Identifying Common Challenges

One of the most common challenges individuals encounter when using affirmations is resistance. This resistance can manifest as inner skepticism, doubt, or disbelief in the effectiveness of affirmations. When faced with resistance, it's essential to acknowledge and explore the underlying beliefs or fears that may be holding you back. Are there deep-seated beliefs about unworthiness or lack that are undermining your confidence in the affirmation process? By shining a light on these limiting beliefs and reframing them into more empowering narratives, you can neutralize resistance and open yourself up to the transformative power of affirmations.

Another common challenge is doubt, which can arise when the desired outcomes seem distant or unattainable. In moments of doubt, it's crucial to remind yourself of the inherent potential within you and the unlimited possibilities of the universe. Trust in the process and reaffirm your commitment to your affirmations, knowing that every repetition strengthens the neural pathways associated with your desired outcomes. Remember that doubt is a natural part of the journey, but it doesn't have to dictate your reality. Choose faith over fear and keep moving forward with unwavering determination.

Practical Strategies for Overcoming Challenges

When faced with challenges in your affirmation practice, it's essential to have a toolbox of practical strategies to overcome them. One effective strategy is reframing negative beliefs into positive affirmations. Instead of focusing on what you lack or fear, reframe your affirmations to focus on what you desire and deserve. For example, if you catch yourself thinking, "I'll never be successful," reframe it into "I am worthy of success, and I attract abundance into my life effortlessly." By consciously shifting your thoughts and language, you empower yourself to rewrite the script of your reality.

Another powerful strategy is using affirmations in conjunction with visualization. Visualization is a complementary practice that amplifies the effectiveness of affirmations by engaging the imagination and emotions. When you visualize yourself experiencing the outcomes you desire while affirming positive statements, you create a powerful synergy that accelerates the manifestation process. Take time each day to visualize yourself living your dreams with vivid detail and emotion, anchoring these visions in your subconscious mind and aligning with their energy.

Incorporating affirmations into your daily routines is another effective strategy for overcoming challenges and staying consistent in your practice. By integrating affirmations into activities you already do regularly, such as brushing your teeth, exercising, or commuting to work, you make them a natural and effortless part of your daily life. Set reminders on your phone or write affirmations on sticky notes placed in prominent locations to keep them top of mind throughout the day. Consistency is key, so commit to practicing affirmations daily, even if it's just for a few minutes each day.

Emphasizing Persistence and Patience

Perhaps the most important aspect of overcoming challenges in your affirmation practice is cultivating persistence and patience. Rome wasn't built in a day, and neither are our dreams. Manifestation is a journey, not a destination, and it requires dedication, resilience, and trust in the process. Stay committed to your affirmation practice, even when the results may not be immediately apparent. Trust that every repetition of your affirmations strengthens the foundation of your beliefs and brings you one step closer to your desired outcomes.

In moments of frustration or setback, remind yourself of how far you've come and the progress you've made. Celebrate even the smallest victories and milestones along the way, knowing that each one brings you closer to your ultimate goals. Remember that setbacks are not failures but opportunities for growth and learning. Stay patient with yourself and the process, knowing that the seeds you're planting with your affirmations will blossom in their own time.

Overcoming common challenges in your affirmation practice requires courage, resilience, and a willingness to embrace the journey of transformation. By identifying and addressing resistance, doubt, and inconsistency with practical strategies and a mindset of persistence and patience, you can navigate any obstacle that comes your way and unlock the full potential of affirmations to manifest your dreams. Trust in yourself, trust in the process, and trust in the power of affirmations to guide you toward the life you desire.

Mastering Manifestation

In the journey of self-discovery and manifestation, mastering the art of affirmations is akin to unlocking the keys to the universe. While traditional affirmations are powerful in their own right, advanced affirmation techniques offer a deeper level of transformation, tapping into the subconscious mind with precision and intention. In this article, we'll explore advanced techniques for enhancing the effectiveness of affirmations, providing step-by-step instructions and real-life success stories to inspire and empower you on your path to personal growth and manifestation.

Exploring Advanced Techniques

One advanced technique for enhancing the effectiveness of affirmations is scripting. Scripting involves writing out your desires as if they have already manifested, in the form of a narrative or journal entry. By vividly describing your desired outcomes in detail, you engage your imagination and emotions, amplifying the power of your affirmations. To implement scripting into your affirmation practice, set aside dedicated time each day to write out your scripted affirmations, focusing on the emotions and sensations associated with your desired outcomes. Allow yourself to immerse fully in the experience, suspending disbelief and allowing the magic of manifestation to unfold.

Another powerful technique is mirror work, which involves affirming positive statements while looking at yourself in the mirror. Mirror work is a potent tool for cultivating self-love, confidence, and self-acceptance, as it invites you to confront and transform any negative self-talk or beliefs. To practice mirror work, stand in front of a mirror and look into your own eyes, repeating affirmations such as "I love and accept myself unconditionally" or "I am worthy of all the blessings life has to offer." Allow yourself to feel the emotions arising within you as you affirm these statements, embracing the truth of your inherent worthiness and beauty.

Incorporating gratitude into your affirmation practice is another advanced technique for amplifying its effectiveness. Gratitude is a powerful vibration that aligns you with the energy of abundance and attracts more blessings into your life. To integrate gratitude into your affirmations, begin each affirmation with a statement of gratitude, such as "I am grateful for the abundance that surrounds me" or "I am thankful for the opportunities that come my way." By infusing your affirmations with gratitude, you shift your focus from lack to abundance, opening yourself up to receive more blessings and miracles.

Implementing Advanced Techniques

To implement scripting into your affirmation practice, follow these steps:

> Set aside dedicated time each day to write out your scripted affirmations.

> Begin by envisioning your desired outcomes in vivid detail, using all your senses to immerse yourself in the experience.

> Write out your affirmations as if they have already manifested, focusing on the emotions and sensations associated with your desired outcomes.

> Read your scripted affirmations aloud or silently, allowing yourself to fully embody the feelings of gratitude, joy, and abundance.

To practice mirror work, follow these steps:

> Find a quiet space where you can be alone with a mirror.

> Stand in front of the mirror and look into your own eyes.

> Repeat positive affirmations aloud or silently, focusing on the emotions and sensations they evoke within you.

> Allow yourself to fully embrace the truth of your affirmations, affirming your worthiness and deservingness of all the blessings life has to offer.

To integrate gratitude into your affirmations, follow these steps:

> Begin each affirmation with a statement of gratitude, expressing thanks for the blessings you already have.

Focus on the positive aspects of your life and the things you are thankful for, no matter how big or small.

Allow yourself to feel the emotions of gratitude deeply as you affirm your desires, knowing that the universe responds to the energy you emit.

Real-life success stories serve as powerful reminders of the transformative power of advanced affirmation techniques. One example is the story of Sarah, who used scripting to manifest her dream job. By scripting her affirmations with clarity, conviction, and gratitude, Sarah was able to align with the energy of her desired outcome and attract the perfect job opportunity into her life. Another example is the story of John, who practiced mirror work to overcome his self-doubt and insecurity. Through daily mirror affirmations, John was able to cultivate a deep sense of self-love and confidence, transforming his relationship with himself and others.

These success stories illustrate the profound impact that advanced affirmation techniques can have on every aspect of our lives, from career and relationships to health and abundance. By embracing these techniques with an open heart and mind, you open yourself up to infinite possibilities for personal growth, transformation, and manifestation. As you incorporate scripting, mirror work, and gratitude into your affirmation practice, watch as your reality begins to mirror your deepest desires, and your dreams unfold with effortless ease and grace.

Chapter 6: Taking Inspired Action

In the journey of manifestation, the power of thought and intention often takes center stage. We're encouraged to visualize our goals, affirm our desires, and align our energy with what we wish to attract into our lives. While these practices are undeniably potent, they're only part of the equation. The missing piece? Action.

Welcome to Chapter 6 of our manifestation blueprint: Taking Inspired Action. In this pivotal chapter, we'll delve into the transformative role that action plays in bringing our dreams into reality. We'll explore the difference between inspired action and random effort, learn strategies for overcoming procrastination, and uncover the inner resistance that may be holding us back. By the end of this chapter, you'll be equipped with the tools and mindset necessary to take consistent steps toward your goals and manifest the life you desire.

Action is the bridge between our inner world of thoughts and intentions and the external world of manifestation. Without action, our dreams remain ethereal and unfulfilled. It's through action that we anchor our intentions into reality, signaling to the universe our commitment and readiness to receive. Whether it's taking a small step or a giant leap, each action we take brings us closer to our desired outcomes.

Not all actions are created equal. Inspired action is driven by intuition, alignment, and passion. It's action that arises from a deep sense of inner knowing and is guided by our highest good. In contrast, random effort is action taken without purpose or alignment, often driven by fear, doubt, or societal pressures. Distinguishing between the two is crucial in ensuring that our actions are in harmony with our intentions and aspirations.

Procrastination is the silent killer of dreams, robbing us of precious time and opportunities. Whether it's fear of failure, overwhelm, or perfectionism, procrastination can manifest in many forms and derail our progress. In this section, we'll explore practical strategies for overcoming procrastination and taking consistent steps toward our goals. From breaking tasks into smaller, manageable steps to setting deadlines and creating accountability systems, we'll discover how to outsmart procrastination and reclaim our power to act.

But what if procrastination is merely a symptom of a deeper issue? What if there's an inner resistance holding us back from taking action? In this part of the chapter, we'll shine a light on the various forms of inner resistance that may be lurking beneath the surface. Whether it's fear, self-doubt, or limiting beliefs, we'll learn how to identify and overcome these obstacles that stand in the way of our success. Through introspection, self-awareness, and self-compassion, we'll untangle the knots of resistance and pave the way for inspired action.

Taking inspired action requires more than just a single burst of effort; it requires a mindset of persistence and resilience. Setbacks and challenges are inevitable on the path to manifestation, but it's how we respond to them that determines our success. In this final section, we'll explore the qualities of persistence and resilience and discover how to cultivate them in our own lives. By reframing setbacks as learning opportunities, practicing gratitude, and celebrating progress, we'll fortify our mindset and navigate the inevitable twists and turns of the manifestation journey with grace and determination.

As we embark on this exploration of taking inspired action, let us remember that each step we take, no matter how small, brings us closer to our dreams. With intention, alignment, and a willingness to take action, we possess the power to manifest miracles in our lives. So let's roll up our sleeves, trust in the process, and take inspired action toward the life we truly desire.

The Power of Action: Building Bridges to Manifestation

In the realm of manifestation, action serves as the cornerstone upon which dreams are built. While visualization, affirmations, and aligning with the universe's energy are essential components of the process, it's through action that we bring our desires from the realm of the possible to the realm of the tangible. In this article, we'll explore the pivotal role that action plays in manifestation, bridging the gap between intention and reality, and exemplifying its transformative power through real-life success stories.

Manifestation begins with a thought, a desire, a dream whispered to the universe. Yet, as powerful as our intentions may be, they remain inert without the catalyst of action. Action is the force that propels our dreams forward, transforming them from ethereal aspirations into concrete manifestations. It is through action that we demonstrate our commitment, determination, and readiness to receive the abundance that awaits us. Without action, our dreams remain mere fantasies, forever out of reach.

Action serves as the bridge that spans the chasm between our intentions and their realization. While visualization and affirmations set the stage and align our energy with our desires, it's through action that we step onto the path of manifestation and begin to traverse it. Action imbues our intentions with substance, giving them form and substance in the physical realm. Each step we take, no matter how small, brings us closer to our goals, building momentum and momentum until we find ourselves standing in the midst of our dreams made manifest.

Consider the aspiring entrepreneur who dreams of launching a successful business. She visualizes her goals, affirms her belief in her abilities, and aligns her energy with the universe's abundance. But without action, her dreams will remain just that—dreams. It's through action—researching her market, developing her product, reaching out to potential clients—that she turns her vision into reality. Each action she takes brings her closer to her goal until, one day, she finds herself at the helm of a thriving business, living the life she once only imagined.

Countless success stories attest to the transformative power of action in the manifestation process. Take, for example, the story of Sarah, who dreamed of traveling the world but felt trapped by her nine-to-five job. Through visualization and affirmations, she clarified her intention to live a life of adventure and freedom. But it wasn't until she took the bold step of quitting her job, booking a one-way ticket to her first destination, and embracing uncertainty that her dreams began to materialize. With each country she explored, each new experience she embraced, Sarah felt her sense of liberation grow until she realized she was living the life she had always dreamed of—all because she took inspired action.

Similarly, consider the story of Michael, who dreamed of writing a bestselling novel but struggled to find the time amidst his busy schedule. Through visualization and affirmations, he affirmed his belief in his writing abilities and his desire to share his story with the world. But it wasn't until he committed to writing for just fifteen minutes a day, no matter what, that he began to see progress. With each word he wrote, each page he completed, Michael felt his confidence grow until, one day, he held his published book in his hands—a testament to the power of consistent action.

In the journey of manifestation, action is the engine that drives us forward, propelling us toward our dreams with unwavering determination and resolve. It is through action that we bridge the gap between intention and manifestation, transforming our desires into reality one step at a time. As we harness the power of action in our own lives, let us remember that each step we take brings us closer to the life we envision, and each action we undertake is a testament to our commitment to living our dreams.

Navigating Inspired Action vs. Random Effort

In the dance of manifestation, action takes center stage as a crucial partner, moving us closer to our dreams with each step we take. Yet, not all actions are created equal. Some propel us forward with purpose and clarity, while others leave us spinning in circles, unsure of our direction. In this article, we'll explore the distinction between inspired action and random effort, shedding light on their defining characteristics and providing examples to illustrate their differences.

Inspired action is the embodiment of intention, guided by intuition, alignment, and passion. It arises from a deep wellspring of inner knowing, a sense of clarity and purpose that transcends logic and reason. Inspired action is in perfect harmony with our deepest desires and aspirations, propelling us forward with a sense of joy, ease, and flow. When we take inspired action, we feel energized, invigorated, and aligned with the universe's abundant flow.

Contrastingly, random effort lacks purpose and alignment, akin to a ship adrift in a vast ocean without a compass or destination. It's action taken for the sake of action, driven by external pressures, fears, or insecurities rather than inner guidance. Random effort leaves us feeling drained, frustrated, and disconnected from our true selves and our deepest desires. It's like spinning our wheels in mud, expending energy without making any meaningful progress toward our goals.

To illustrate the distinction between inspired action and random effort, let's consider the example of Sarah, a budding artist who dreams of sharing her creations with the world. Inspired by her passion for painting and her desire to inspire others, Sarah feels a deep sense of alignment with her artistic journey. When she picks up her brush and begins to paint, she does so with a sense of joy and purpose, allowing her intuition to guide her brushstrokes and her heart to infuse her work with meaning. Each stroke is imbued with intention, each color chosen with care, as Sarah loses herself in the creative flow.

Now, let's contrast Sarah's experience with that of Alex, who also dreams of becoming an artist but struggles with self-doubt and insecurity. Fueled by the pressure to succeed and the fear of failure, Alex approaches his art with a sense of urgency and desperation. He paints frantically, seeking validation and approval from others, but his work lacks soul and authenticity. Despite his efforts, he feels disconnected from his creativity and his true passion, leaving him feeling empty and unfulfilled.

Consider the story of Jenna, who dreams of starting her own business but feels paralyzed by fear and self-doubt. Despite her passion and determination, she finds herself hesitating to take the necessary steps to turn her dream into reality. Then, one day, she has a sudden moment of clarity—a flash of inspiration that lights up her path forward. With newfound confidence and conviction, Jenna takes inspired action, reaching out to potential clients, networking with fellow entrepreneurs, and laying the groundwork for her business with purpose and intention. As she moves forward on her journey, she feels a sense of alignment and empowerment, knowing that she is on the right path toward realizing her dreams.

In contrast, consider the story of Mike, who also dreams of starting his own business but approaches the process with a sense of desperation and urgency. Fueled by external pressures and the fear of failure, he throws himself into his work, taking action for the sake of action without stopping to consider whether it's aligned with his true desires and values. Despite his tireless efforts, Mike finds himself spinning his wheels, unable to gain traction or make meaningful progress toward his goals. Exhausted and disillusioned, he wonders why success seems to elude him despite all his hard work.

In the dance of manifestation, the distinction between inspired action and random effort is crucial. Inspired action is the key that unlocks the door to our dreams, guiding us toward our highest potential with grace and ease. Random effort, on the other hand, leads us down winding paths that ultimately lead nowhere, leaving us feeling drained, frustrated, and disconnected from our true selves. By cultivating a deep sense of alignment with our desires and allowing our intuition to guide our actions, we can navigate the journey of manifestation with clarity, purpose, and joy.

Strategies for Taking Consistent Steps Toward Your Goals

Procrastination—a word that strikes fear into the hearts of dreamers and achievers alike. It's the silent saboteur that lurks in the shadows, whispering seductively in our ears, tempting us to put off today what we can do tomorrow. Yet, despite its pervasive presence, procrastination is not insurmountable. In this article, we'll explore the common reasons behind procrastination, provide practical techniques for overcoming it, and offer guidance on how to cultivate consistency in action-taking, allowing you to move confidently toward your goals with purpose and determination.

Before we can tackle procrastination head-on, it's essential to understand its roots. Procrastination often stems from a variety of sources, including fear of failure, overwhelm, perfectionism, and lack of clarity or motivation. We may procrastinate because the task ahead seems daunting, or because we're afraid of making mistakes or falling short of our expectations. Sometimes, procrastination is simply a way of avoiding discomfort or uncertainty, opting for short-term pleasure over long-term progress. By identifying the underlying reasons for our procrastination, we can begin to address them effectively and reclaim our power to act.

Once we've identified the root causes of our procrastination, it's time to roll up our sleeves and get to work. One effective strategy for overcoming procrastination is to break tasks down into smaller, more manageable steps. By breaking a daunting task into bite-sized chunks, we make it easier to get started and build momentum gradually. Setting deadlines and creating accountability systems can also help keep procrastination at bay, providing a sense of urgency and external motivation to stay on track. Additionally, we can harness the power of visualization and positive self-talk to reframe our mindset and cultivate a sense of confidence and determination.

Consistency is the key to success in any endeavor. Yet, cultivating consistency in action-taking can be challenging, especially in the face of competing priorities and distractions. One effective strategy for cultivating consistency is to establish routines and rituals that support our goals and priorities. By incorporating daily habits and practices into our lives, we create a framework for success, ensuring that we make progress toward our goals each day, no matter how small. Prioritizing tasks and setting clear boundaries can also help us stay focused and avoid the trap of procrastination, allowing us to allocate our time and energy effectively.

Procrastination may be a formidable foe, but it is not invincible. By understanding the root causes of procrastination, implementing practical techniques for overcoming it, and cultivating consistency in action-taking, we can break free from its grip and move confidently toward our goals. With determination, discipline, and a willingness to take consistent steps forward, we can overcome procrastination and achieve our dreams with clarity, purpose, and unwavering resolve.

Strategies to Overcome Your Inner Demons

Inner resistance—a formidable adversary that often lurks in the shadows, silently sabotaging our efforts and holding us back from realizing our full potential. It manifests in various forms, from the insidious whispers of fear and self-doubt to the suffocating grip of limiting beliefs. Yet, despite its stealthy nature, inner resistance is not insurmountable. In this article, we'll shine a light on the different faces of inner resistance, offer practical strategies for identifying and addressing it, and underscore the importance of self-awareness and self-compassion in overcoming its grip.

Inner resistance can take many forms, each with its own unique flavor of self-sabotage. Fear, perhaps the most primal and pervasive form of inner resistance, manifests as a paralyzing force that keeps us trapped in our comfort zones, afraid to venture into the unknown. Self-doubt whispers cruelly in our ears, questioning our worthiness and capabilities, and undermining our confidence. Limiting beliefs, deeply ingrained patterns of thought and perception, act as invisible shackles, constraining our potential and keeping us tethered to the past. These are but a few of the guises that inner resistance may wear, each presenting its own set of challenges to overcome.

To overcome inner resistance, we must first shine a light on the shadows where it hides. One effective strategy for identifying inner resistance is journaling, which allows us to explore our thoughts and emotions with honesty and clarity. By writing freely and without judgment, we can uncover the underlying fears, doubts, and limiting beliefs that hold us back. Mindfulness practices, such as meditation and deep breathing exercises, can also help us cultivate awareness of our inner landscape, allowing us to observe our thoughts and emotions without getting swept away by them. Additionally, seeking support from mentors or coaches who can provide guidance, encouragement, and accountability can be invaluable in navigating the murky waters of inner resistance.

In our journey to overcome inner resistance, self-awareness is our most potent weapon. By cultivating a deep understanding of our thoughts, emotions, and patterns of behavior, we can begin to untangle the knots of resistance that bind us. Yet, self-awareness alone is not enough—we must also cultivate self-compassion, extending kindness and understanding to ourselves in the face of inner turmoil. Rather than berating ourselves for our perceived shortcomings or failures, we can offer ourselves the same compassion and support that we would offer to a dear friend facing similar challenges. Through self-awareness and self-compassion, we can navigate the turbulent waters of inner resistance with grace and resilience, emerging stronger and more empowered on the other side.

Inner resistance may be a formidable foe, but it is not unbeatable. By shining a light on the shadows where it hides, offering strategies for identifying and addressing it, and cultivating self-awareness and self-compassion, we can overcome its grip and reclaim our power to create the life we desire. With courage, perseverance, and a willingness to confront our inner demons, we can break free from the chains of resistance and step into our fullest potential with clarity, purpose, and unwavering resolve.

Chapter 7: The Law of Detachment

This chapter, delves into the transformative concept of detachment—a principle that challenges our instinctual desire to control outcomes and invites us to surrender to the flow of life. As we explore the depths of detachment, we'll uncover its profound influence on our ability to manifest our desires with clarity, ease, and grace.

Detachment, contrary to common belief, is not about indifference or apathy. Instead, it's a profound act of trust and surrender—a willingness to release our grip on specific outcomes and embrace the unknown with open arms. By letting go of attachment to how things "should" unfold, we open ourselves up to the infinite possibilities that lie beyond our limited perceptions.

Throughout this chapter, we'll unravel the mysteries of detachment, exploring how the simple act of letting go can lead to profound transformation in our lives. We'll discover how detachment fosters greater receptivity to the universe's guidance, allowing synchronicities and serendipities to unfold effortlessly. We'll learn practical exercises and techniques to cultivate detachment in our daily lives, empowering us to release resistance and embrace the flow of abundance.

So, prepare to embark on a journey of liberation and empowerment as we dive into the Law of Detachment. By embracing the power of letting go, we unlock the door to a life filled with joy, fulfilment, and infinite possibilities. Let's begin our exploration and discover the magic that awaits us on the path of detachment.

Embracing Detachment

In the pursuit of our dreams and desires, we often find ourselves caught in a delicate dance between action and surrender. While taking inspired action is essential in the manifestation process, equally important is the ability to let go of attachment to specific outcomes and surrender to the flow of life. This is where the concept of detachment comes into play—a powerful principle that holds the key to unlocking the magic of manifestation.

At its core, detachment is about releasing our grip on specific outcomes and trusting in the wisdom of the universe. It's a radical act of surrender—an acknowledgment that we are not in control of the intricate web of events that unfold in our lives. Instead of clinging to a predetermined vision of how things should be, detachment invites us to surrender to the infinite possibilities that lie beyond our limited perceptions. It's about letting go of the need to micromanage every aspect of our lives and embracing the unknown with open arms.

Detachment is not synonymous with indifference or resignation. Rather, it's a profound act of trust—a willingness to surrender to the flow of life and embrace whatever comes our way with equanimity and grace. When we release attachment to specific outcomes, we free ourselves from the chains of expectation and allow room for miracles to unfold. Detachment is about surrendering our need for control and placing our faith in the universe's infinite wisdom and benevolence.

One of the most powerful aspects of detachment is its ability to cultivate flexibility and openness in our lives. When we're attached to a specific outcome, we tend to narrow our focus and shut ourselves off from the myriad possibilities that exist beyond our limited vision. Detachment, on the other hand, opens the door to infinite possibilities, allowing us to remain flexible and adaptable in the face of uncertainty. It's about trusting that whatever unfolds is for our highest good, even if it deviates from our original plans.

Detachment also fosters a deeper sense of receptivity to the universe's guidance. When we release attachment to specific outcomes, we become more attuned to the subtle whispers of intuition and the synchronicities that guide us along our path. Instead of forcing our will upon the world, we allow ourselves to be guided by a higher intelligence—one that knows far more than we could ever comprehend. Detachment opens the door to serendipity, allowing miracles to unfold in ways we could never have imagined.

In the journey of manifestation, detachment is a potent ally—a guiding light that illuminates the path forward with clarity and grace. By releasing attachment to specific outcomes and surrendering to the flow of life, we unlock the door to infinite possibilities and invite miracles to unfold effortlessly. So let us embrace the power of detachment, trusting in the wisdom of the universe and surrendering to the magic that awaits us on the journey of manifestation.

How Detachment Leads to Manifestation Success

In the pursuit of our goals and desires, we're often taught that success comes from relentless effort, unwavering focus, and a firm grip on our objectives. Yet, paradoxically, it's often when we loosen our hold and surrender to the flow of life that we truly unlock the magic of manifestation. In this article, we'll explore the transformative nature of letting go and how it can lead to better results in our manifestation journey. Through examples and anecdotes, we'll witness the profound impact of detachment in achieving desired outcomes, and we'll uncover how releasing attachment to specific results allows for the natural unfolding of events, paving the way for manifestation success.

At first glance, the idea of letting go may seem counterintuitive—how can surrendering control lead to greater success? Yet, it's in this act of release that we create space for miracles to occur. When we cling tightly to our desires, we inadvertently create resistance, pushing away the very outcomes we seek. It's only when we release our attachment to specific results that we allow the universe to work its magic, orchestrating events in ways we could never have imagined. Letting go is not about giving up or resigning ourselves to fate; it's about trusting in the natural flow of life and surrendering to the infinite possibilities that lie beyond our limited perceptions.

Countless stories and anecdotes serve as testament to the transformative power of detachment in achieving manifestation success. Take, for example, the story of Sarah, who spent years desperately chasing after a promotion at work, only to find herself overlooked time and time again. It wasn't until she finally let go of her attachment to the outcome and focused instead on doing her best work without expectation that she received the recognition she had long desired. Similarly, John had spent years pining for a romantic partner, only to find himself disappointed time and time again. It wasn't until he released his attachment to finding love and focused instead on cultivating self-love and fulfilment that he attracted the perfect partner into his life. These stories serve as powerful reminders that when we release attachment to specific outcomes, we open ourselves up to a world of infinite possibilities, allowing for the manifestation of our deepest desires.

When we cling tightly to our desires, we create resistance, blocking the flow of abundance and limiting our manifestation potential. It's like trying to swim against the current—we exhaust ourselves in the process and make little progress toward our goals. However, when we release attachment and surrender to the flow of life, we reduce resistance and allow for the natural unfolding of events. Opportunities begin to present themselves effortlessly, synchronicities abound, and our desires manifest with ease. Letting go is not about passive resignation; it's about actively participating in the co-creation process with the universe, trusting that everything is unfolding exactly as it should.

In the journey of manifestation, letting go is a powerful tool that can lead to greater success and fulfilment. By releasing attachment to specific outcomes, we create space for miracles to occur and allow for the natural unfolding of events. So let us loosen our grip, trust in the wisdom of the universe, and surrender to the flow of life. In doing so, we invite abundance, joy, and manifestation success to flow effortlessly into our lives.

Practical Exercises for Cultivating Detachment

In the journey of manifestation, one of the most powerful skills we can cultivate is the art of letting go. Detachment allows us to release attachment to specific outcomes and surrender to the flow of life, opening the door to greater manifestation success and inner peace. In this article, we'll explore practical exercises and techniques to help readers cultivate detachment in their daily lives, guiding them on a journey of liberation and empowerment.

Cultivating Detachment in Daily Life

Detachment begins with awareness—becoming mindful of our attachments and learning to release them with grace and ease. One simple yet effective exercise is to practice non-attachment in daily activities. Start by consciously letting go of small attachments throughout the day, such as preferences for how things should be or the need for approval from others. Notice any resistance that arises and gently release it, allowing yourself to remain open and receptive to whatever unfolds.

Guided Meditation and Visualization Exercises

Guided meditation and visualization are powerful tools for releasing attachment to specific outcomes and surrendering to the flow of life. Begin by finding a quiet space where you can relax and focus your attention inward. Then, visualize yourself letting go of any attachments or expectations you may be holding onto. See yourself releasing these attachments with love and compassion, allowing them to float away like clouds in the sky. As you let go, feel a sense of lightness and freedom wash over you, knowing that you are surrendering to the infinite wisdom of the universe.

Journal Prompts for Reflection

Journaling is another powerful practice for cultivating detachment and releasing attachment to limiting beliefs or fears. Set aside time each day to reflect on any attachments or expectations you may be holding onto. Then, write them down in your journal, exploring the underlying beliefs or fears that may be driving them. Once you've identified these attachments, write a letter to yourself, releasing them with love and compassion. Affirm that you are worthy and deserving of all the abundance the universe has to offer, and trust that everything is unfolding exactly as it should.

Mindfulness Practices for Letting Go

Mindfulness practices are invaluable for cultivating present-moment awareness and letting go of the need to control outcomes. One simple mindfulness exercise is to practice "surfing the waves" of your emotions. Instead of resisting or suppressing uncomfortable emotions, allow yourself to fully experience them without judgment. Notice the sensations in your body and the thoughts in your mind, observing them with curiosity and compassion. As you practice mindfulness, you'll begin to cultivate a sense of inner peace and acceptance, allowing you to release attachment and surrender to the flow of life.

In the journey of manifestation, detachment is a vital skill that empowers us to release attachment to specific outcomes and surrender to the infinite possibilities of the universe. By practicing these exercises and techniques, readers can cultivate a sense of inner peace and empowerment, allowing them to navigate the ups and downs of life with grace and ease. So let us embrace the art of letting go, knowing that in surrendering to the flow of life, we open ourselves up to greater abundance, joy, and manifestation success.

The Keys to Manifestation Mastery

In the intricate dance of manifestation, trust and surrender play pivotal roles, guiding us along the path to our deepest desires. In this article, we'll explore the profound interplay between trust, surrender, and detachment, uncovering how these qualities pave the way for abundance, joy, and manifestation success.

Trust is the bedrock upon which manifestation flourishes, providing the fertile soil in which our desires can take root and bloom. When we trust in the universe's inherent wisdom and benevolence, we relinquish the need to control outcomes and surrender to the flow of life. Trust allows us to release attachment to specific results and embrace the unknown with open arms, knowing that everything is unfolding exactly as it should. Cultivating trust involves surrendering the illusion of control and placing our faith in the unseen forces that guide our journey.

Surrender is the gentle art of releasing resistance and allowing for the natural unfolding of events. When we surrender, we let go of the need to micromanage every aspect of our lives and instead trust in the divine timing of the universe. Surrender is not about giving up or resigning ourselves to fate; it's about embracing the flow of life and surrendering to the infinite possibilities that lie beyond our limited perceptions. In releasing resistance, we create space for abundance and opportunities to flow effortlessly into our lives.

Cultivating trust and surrender is a practice—an ongoing journey of letting go and surrendering to the wisdom of the universe. Affirmations and visualization are powerful tools for cultivating trust, allowing us to reaffirm our belief in the universe's abundant nature and our inherent worthiness to receive. Affirmations such as "I trust in the divine timing of the universe" and "I surrender to the flow of life" can help to reprogram our subconscious mind and align our energy with the frequency of trust and surrender.

Visualization is another potent practice for cultivating trust and surrender, allowing us to envision ourselves releasing attachment to specific outcomes and surrendering to the flow of life. By visualizing ourselves letting go of resistance and embracing the unknown with open arms, we create a powerful energetic shift that aligns us with the manifestation of our desires.

Letting go of the need for certainty is another crucial aspect of cultivating trust and surrender. Instead of clinging to rigid expectations and outcomes, we can practice letting go of attachment and embracing the beauty of uncertainty. In doing so, we open ourselves up to a world of infinite possibilities, allowing abundance and opportunities to flow effortlessly into our lives.

In the journey of manifestation, trust, surrender, and detachment are the guiding principles that lead us to our deepest desires. By cultivating trust in the universe's wisdom, surrendering to the flow of life, and releasing attachment to specific outcomes, we open ourselves up to a world of infinite possibilities and manifestation success. So let us embrace the art of trust and surrender, knowing that in releasing resistance, we invite abundance, joy, and fulfilment to flow effortlessly into our lives.

Detachment: The Path to Inner Peace and Fulfilment

In the hustle and bustle of modern life, finding a sense of inner peace and fulfilment can often feel like an elusive dream. Yet, paradoxically, it's often when we release attachment to external outcomes and surrender to the flow of life that we find the greatest sense of peace and fulfilment. In this article, we'll explore the profound connection between detachment and inner peace, uncovering how letting go of attachment fosters a deep sense of tranquility and freedom from external pressures. We'll also delve into how detachment leads to greater fulfilment by allowing us to focus on the present moment and find joy in the journey, rather than fixating on future outcomes. Finally, we'll offer practical practices for cultivating gratitude, mindfulness, and acceptance to deepen the sense of detachment and inner peace in our lives.

Detachment is the art of releasing attachment to specific outcomes and surrendering to the flow of life. When we detach from external expectations and outcomes, we free ourselves from the burden of constantly striving to meet societal standards or chasing after elusive goals. Instead, we find peace in the present moment, knowing that we are exactly where we need to be. Detachment allows us to let go of the need for external validation and find a sense of inner peace that comes from within.

Detachment fosters a sense of freedom from the pressures of external expectations by allowing us to release the need to control outcomes. When we detach from the outcomes we desire, we no longer feel compelled to mold ourselves to fit into a particular mold or live up to others' standards. Instead, we embrace our authentic selves and find peace in simply being who we are. Detachment liberates us from the constraints of society's expectations and empowers us to live life on our own terms.

Detachment is also closely linked to greater fulfilment, as it allows us to focus on the present moment and find joy in the journey, rather than fixating on future outcomes. When we release attachment to specific results, we open ourselves up to a world of infinite possibilities and opportunities. We become more present and engaged in our lives, savoring each moment and finding fulfilment in the simple pleasures of everyday life. Detachment shifts our focus from the destination to the journey, allowing us to find joy and fulfilment in the process of becoming.

Cultivating gratitude, mindfulness, and acceptance are powerful practices for deepening the sense of detachment and inner peace in our lives. Gratitude helps us to shift our focus from what we lack to what we have, fostering a sense of abundance and contentment. Mindfulness allows us to fully engage with the present moment, letting go of worries about the past or future. Acceptance teaches us to embrace life as it is, without judgment or resistance, allowing us to find peace amidst the chaos.

In embracing detachment, we open ourselves up to a world of inner peace and fulfilment. By releasing attachment to external outcomes, we free ourselves from the pressures of society's expectations and find joy in the present moment. Through practices such as gratitude, mindfulness, and acceptance, we deepen our sense of detachment and cultivate a profound sense of inner peace that radiates from within. So let us embrace the path of detachment, knowing that in letting go, we find true freedom and fulfilment.

Deepening the Connection Between Detachment and Inner Peace

As we delve deeper into the realm of detachment, we uncover its profound connection to inner peace and fulfilment. Detachment invites us to relinquish our grip on the reins of control and surrender to the natural flow of life. In doing so, we release the burden of incessant striving and instead find solace in the tranquility of the present moment. By detaching from the relentless pursuit of external validation or material gain, we discover a profound sense of inner peace that transcends worldly desires.

Detachment liberates us from the shackles of external pressures, allowing us to break free from the confines of societal expectations. When we cease striving to conform to predefined notions of success or happiness, we liberate ourselves to chart our own unique path. Detachment empowers us to embrace our authentic selves, liberated from the constraints of comparison or judgment. In this newfound freedom, we discover the true essence of fulfilment – the freedom to be unapologetically ourselves.

Detachment redirects our focus from the destination to the journey itself, enabling us to find fulfilment in the process of becoming. Instead of fixating on distant goals or future outcomes, we immerse ourselves fully in the richness of each moment. We savor the small victories, relish in the beauty of everyday experiences, and find joy in the simple pleasures of life. Detachment teaches us that fulfilment is not a destination to be reached but a state of being cultivated along the journey.

To deepen our sense of detachment and inner peace, we can incorporate practical tools and techniques into our daily lives. Gratitude practice allows us to shift our perspective from scarcity to abundance, fostering a profound sense of contentment with what we have. Mindfulness practice invites us to anchor ourselves in the present moment, releasing attachment to past regrets or future anxieties. Acceptance practice teaches us to embrace life as it unfolds, surrendering to the ebb and flow of existence with grace and equanimity.

In embracing the journey of detachment, we embark on a profound quest for inner peace and fulfilment. We learn to release attachment to external outcomes and surrender to the wisdom of the universe, trusting in the inherent order of life. Through the practice of detachment, we discover the true essence of freedom – the freedom to live authentically, to embrace uncertainty, and to find joy in the beauty of each moment. So let us embark on this transformative journey of detachment, knowing that in letting go, we find the ultimate liberation and fulfilment.

Chapter 8: Dealing with Challenges and Setbacks

As we delve into the complexities of manifesting our deepest desires, it's essential to acknowledge that the path is not always smooth. Just as in any journey of growth and transformation, challenges and setbacks are inevitable companions along the way. However, it's how we choose to navigate these obstacles that ultimately determines our success.

In this chapter, we'll explore the terrain of adversity and resilience, learning how to confront challenges head-on while maintaining unwavering faith in our ability to manifest our dreams. From acknowledging the inevitability of setbacks to offering practical strategies for overcoming obstacles, we'll arm ourselves with the tools and mindset needed to persevere in the face of adversity.

Our journey into the realm of manifestation begins with a crucial realization: the road to our desires is not always paved with smooth pavement. Despite our best intentions and efforts, we are bound to encounter bumps, detours, and roadblocks along the way. It's essential to accept this reality with grace and humility, understanding that challenges are not signs of failure but rather opportunities for growth and refinement.

As we embark on our manifestation journey, we must embrace the inevitability of setbacks and approach them with an open heart and mind. By acknowledging that manifestation is not always smooth sailing, we free ourselves from the burden of unrealistic expectations and allow space for grace and resilience to flourish.

While challenges may be an unavoidable aspect of the manifestation process, they need not derail us from our path towards success. In this section, we'll explore a range of practical strategies for overcoming obstacles and maintaining positivity in the face of adversity.

From reframing negative beliefs to staying focused on our goals and seeking support from mentors or communities, there are countless ways to navigate challenges with grace and resilience. By arming ourselves with the tools and mindset needed to confront adversity head-on, we empower ourselves to emerge stronger and more resilient than ever before.

No exploration of challenges and setbacks would be complete without the inspiring tales of those who have weathered the storms and emerged victorious on the other side. In this section, we'll shine a spotlight on the stories of resilience and perseverance that serve as beacons of hope and inspiration on our manifestation journey.

From overcoming financial hardships to navigating personal crises, these stories remind us that adversity is not a barrier to success but rather a stepping stone to greatness. By drawing strength and inspiration from those who have walked this path before us, we gain the courage and resilience needed to confront our own challenges head-on.

As we navigate the twists and turns of our manifestation journey, setbacks can serve as invaluable opportunities for growth and self-discovery. In this section, we'll explore the mindset shift needed to view setbacks as catalysts for transformation rather than obstacles to success.

By embracing setbacks as integral parts of the manifestation process, we open ourselves up to a world of growth and possibility. Instead of allowing setbacks to derail us from our path, we can use them as springboards for personal and spiritual evolution, emerging stronger and more resilient than ever before.

At the heart of our ability to navigate challenges and setbacks with grace and resilience lies the practice of self-compassion. In this final section, we'll explore the transformative power of self-compassion in building emotional resilience and fortitude in the face of adversity.

From self-care rituals to self-affirmations and mindfulness practices, there are countless ways to cultivate self-compassion and deepen our resilience in the face of adversity. By learning to treat ourselves with kindness and compassion, we create a foundation of inner strength and resilience that allows us to weather life's storms with grace and dignity.

As we embark on this exploration of challenges and setbacks, let us approach the journey with an open heart and mind, knowing that each obstacle we encounter is an opportunity for growth and transformation. By embracing adversity with courage and resilience, we pave the way for manifestation success beyond our wildest dreams.

Embracing Challenges on the Path to Manifestation Mastery

Embarking on the journey of manifestation is akin to setting sail on a vast ocean of possibilities, guided by the compass of our deepest desires. However, amidst the excitement of setting sail towards our dreams, it's crucial to acknowledge that the voyage will not always be smooth sailing. In fact, challenges and setbacks are an inevitable part of the manifestation journey, each serving as a rite of passage towards our ultimate destination.

As we set forth on our manifestation journey, it's essential to dispel any illusions of smooth sailing and instead prepare ourselves for the inevitable storms that lie ahead. While the concept of manifestation may be shrouded in notions of effortless abundance and instant gratification, the reality is far more nuanced. Just as in any journey of growth and transformation, obstacles are bound to arise, testing our resolve and commitment to our goals.

In the realm of manifestation, there exists a pervasive misconception that success comes easily and effortlessly to those who possess the right mindset or techniques. This misconception often leads individuals to believe that encountering challenges or setbacks is a sign of failure or inadequacy. However, the truth is that manifestation is not a linear process but rather a journey filled with peaks and valleys, each offering valuable lessons and insights along the way.

Rather than viewing challenges as obstacles to be avoided or overcome, it's essential to embrace them as integral parts of the growth process. Each setback we encounter serves as an opportunity for introspection, refinement, and growth, guiding us closer to the realization of our desires. By acknowledging and accepting the inevitability of challenges, we free ourselves from the burden of unrealistic expectations and open ourselves up to the transformative power of adversity.

In the face of challenges and setbacks, our ability to navigate the storms with grace and resilience is paramount. Instead of allowing adversity to derail us from our path, we can choose to confront it head-on, armed with the knowledge that every obstacle we encounter is an opportunity for growth and refinement. By embracing challenges as catalysts for transformation, we cultivate a mindset of resilience and perseverance that propels us forward on our manifestation journey.

Navigating the Path to Manifestation Mastery

In the journey of manifestation, encountering obstacles is not a matter of if, but when. These obstacles can take many forms – from self-doubt and negative beliefs to external challenges and setbacks. However, it's not the presence of obstacles that determines our success, but rather how we choose to navigate through them. Here, we explore practical strategies for overcoming obstacles and maintaining positivity amidst adversity.

One of the most powerful strategies for overcoming obstacles is to reframe negative beliefs. Often, it's our own limiting beliefs and self-doubt that become the biggest barriers on our manifestation journey. By consciously reframing negative thoughts into positive affirmations, we can shift our mindset from one of scarcity to abundance. For example, instead of focusing on what we lack, we can affirm our inherent worthiness and deservingness of success. Through consistent practice, reframing negative beliefs can transform our perception of obstacles into opportunities for growth.

Maintaining focus on our goals is essential when navigating through obstacles. It's easy to become distracted or discouraged when faced with challenges, but by keeping our eyes firmly set on the prize, we can stay motivated and driven to overcome any hurdle that comes our way. Setting clear, actionable goals and breaking them down into smaller, manageable steps can help us maintain momentum and progress, even in the face of adversity. Additionally, regularly revisiting our goals and visualizing our desired outcomes can reinforce our commitment and keep us on track towards manifestation success.

Navigating obstacles alone can be daunting, which is why seeking support from mentors or communities can be invaluable. Whether it's finding a mentor who has walked a similar path and can offer guidance and perspective, or connecting with like-minded individuals in online forums or support groups, surrounding ourselves with a supportive network can provide encouragement, accountability, and fresh insights. By sharing our struggles and triumphs with others, we not only gain valuable support but also realize that we are not alone in our journey.

Maintaining a positive mindset is crucial when faced with adversity. It's easy to succumb to negativity and self-doubt when things don't go as planned, but by consciously choosing to focus on the positive aspects of our journey, we can shift our energy and outlook towards one of optimism and possibility. Practicing gratitude, visualization, and affirmations can help cultivate a positive mindset and remind us of the abundance and blessings that surround us, even in challenging times. By adopting a mindset of positivity and resilience, we can weather any storm with grace and fortitude.

Lastly, managing stress and anxiety is essential for maintaining our well-being and resilience in the face of obstacles. When we're feeling overwhelmed or anxious, it's easy to lose sight of our goals and succumb to negativity. Incorporating stress-reduction techniques such as mindfulness meditation, deep breathing exercises, or physical activity into our daily routine can help calm the mind and body, allowing us to approach challenges with clarity and composure. Additionally, practicing self-care and prioritizing our mental and emotional health can help us build resilience and bounce back stronger from setbacks.

Embracing Adversity: The Path to Manifestation Mastery

In the pursuit of our goals and dreams, setbacks are often seen as stumbling blocks—obstacles to be avoided or overcome as quickly as possible. However, what if we were to shift our perspective and view setbacks not as roadblocks, but as stepping stones on the path to growth and self-improvement? What if, instead of being discouraged by challenges, we embraced them as opportunities to refine our approach and strengthen our resolve?

Learning from setbacks requires a fundamental mindset shift—one that acknowledges adversity not as a hindrance, but as a necessary part of the manifestation journey. This shift begins with recognizing that setbacks are not indicative of failure, but rather serve as valuable lessons in disguise. Each setback presents an opportunity to learn, adapt, and grow, ultimately leading us closer to our desired outcomes.

One practical technique for extracting lessons from setbacks is to approach them with curiosity rather than frustration. Rather than dwelling on what went wrong or assigning blame, ask yourself: What can I learn from this experience? What insights can I gain that will help me navigate similar challenges in the future? Adopting a curious mindset allows you to explore the underlying factors contributing to the setback and uncover valuable insights that can inform your future actions.

Another essential aspect of learning from setbacks is cultivating resilience—the ability to bounce back from adversity stronger and more determined than before. Resilience is not about avoiding setbacks altogether, but rather about developing the inner strength and perseverance to withstand them. Cultivating resilience involves practicing self-care, maintaining a positive outlook, and surrounding yourself with a supportive network of friends, family, and mentors who can offer guidance and encouragement during difficult times.

Moreover, it's important to view setbacks as integral parts of the manifestation process rather than deviations from the path to success. Manifestation is not a linear journey—it's a dynamic, ever-evolving process that involves both triumphs and setbacks. By embracing setbacks as natural elements of this process, you can approach them with a sense of acceptance and equanimity, knowing that each challenge brings with it the opportunity for growth and transformation.

Incorporating setbacks into your manifestation approach requires a willingness to adapt and refine your strategies as you encounter obstacles along the way. Rather than stubbornly clinging to a single course of action, be open to exploring alternative paths and adjusting your tactics based on the lessons learned from setbacks. Flexibility and adaptability are key qualities that enable you to navigate the twists and turns of the manifestation journey with grace and resilience.

Ultimately, learning from setbacks and growing through adversity is not just about achieving your external goals—it's about cultivating inner strength, wisdom, and resilience that will serve you well in all areas of life. By embracing setbacks as opportunities for growth and self-improvement, you can transform challenges into catalysts for personal and spiritual evolution. So the next time you encounter a setback on your manifestation journey, remember to approach it with curiosity, resilience, and an unwavering belief in your ability to overcome any obstacle that stands in your way.

In the pursuit of mastery in any aspect of life, setbacks often serve as unexpected yet invaluable teachers. They challenge our assumptions, push the boundaries of our comfort zones, and ultimately reveal our true strength and resilience. However, the key to unlocking the transformative power of setbacks lies not in merely enduring them, but in actively embracing them as catalysts for growth and self-discovery.

One powerful technique for extracting lessons from setbacks is the practice of mindfulness. By cultivating present-moment awareness and non-judgmental observation, mindfulness allows us to approach setbacks with a sense of clarity and equanimity. Instead of becoming overwhelmed by negative emotions or dwelling on past mistakes, we can simply acknowledge the reality of the situation and explore it with a curious and open mind. In doing so, we create space for insights to arise and wisdom to emerge from even the most challenging experiences.

Furthermore, reframing setbacks as opportunities for creative problem-solving can help shift our mindset from one of defeat to one of empowerment. Rather than viewing setbacks as insurmountable obstacles, we can see them as invitations to think outside the box, experiment with new approaches, and discover innovative solutions. By embracing a spirit of curiosity and experimentation, we not only increase our chances of overcoming setbacks but also uncover hidden strengths and talents that may have otherwise remained dormant.

In addition to mindfulness and creative problem-solving, resilience-building practices such as gratitude, self-compassion, and positive self-talk can further support us in navigating setbacks with grace and resilience. Cultivating gratitude for the lessons learned and the progress made, practicing self-compassion in the face of setbacks, and using affirmations and positive self-talk to bolster our confidence and motivation can all help fortify our inner resilience and empower us to persevere in the face of adversity.

Ultimately, the journey of learning from setbacks and growing through adversity is not a solitary one. It is through the support and encouragement of others that we are able to truly thrive in the face of challenges. Seeking guidance from mentors, sharing our experiences with trusted friends and loved ones, and participating in supportive communities can all provide invaluable sources of strength and inspiration during difficult times. By surrounding ourselves with a supportive network of allies, we not only lighten the burden of setbacks but also amplify the collective wisdom and resilience of the entire community.

Setbacks are not obstacles to be avoided but opportunities to be embraced on the path to manifestation mastery. By approaching setbacks with curiosity, resilience, and a willingness to learn, we can extract valuable lessons, uncover hidden strengths, and ultimately transform challenges into catalysts for growth and self-discovery. Through mindfulness, creative problem-solving, and resilience-building practices, we can navigate setbacks with grace and resilience, emerging stronger, wiser, and more empowered than ever before. So the next time you encounter a setback on your manifestation journey, remember that it is not the end of the road but merely a detour leading you closer to your dreams.

Nurturing Inner Strength: The Power of Self-Compassion and Resilience

In life, adversity is inevitable. Whether it's facing setbacks in our personal or professional lives, dealing with unexpected challenges, or navigating difficult emotions, we all encounter moments of struggle. However, it is not the adversity itself that defines us, but rather how we respond to it. Cultivating self-compassion and resilience is essential for weathering life's storms with grace and inner strength.

Self-compassion, a concept rooted in Buddhist psychology and popularized by Dr. Kristin Neff, is the practice of treating ourselves with kindness, understanding, and acceptance, particularly in times of difficulty or suffering. It involves extending the same compassion and empathy to ourselves that we would offer to a close friend or loved one facing similar challenges. Research has shown that self-compassion is strongly associated with psychological well-being, resilience, and emotional stability, making it a powerful tool for navigating adversity.

One way to cultivate self-compassion is through self-care rituals—intentional practices that nurture our physical, emotional, and spiritual well-being. Whether it's taking a relaxing bath, going for a nature walk, or indulging in a favorite hobby, self-care rituals remind us to prioritize our own needs and replenish our energy reserves. By carving out time for self-care on a regular basis, we not only enhance our resilience to stress but also deepen our sense of self-compassion and self-worth.

In addition to self-care rituals, self-affirmations can also be a powerful tool for cultivating self-compassion and building resilience. Affirmations are positive statements that challenge and replace negative self-talk, helping to reframe our inner dialogue in a more supportive and empowering way. By repeating affirmations such as "I am worthy of love and belonging" or "I trust in my ability to overcome challenges," we reinforce positive beliefs about ourselves and strengthen our inner resilience in the face of adversity.

Mindfulness meditation is another effective practice for cultivating self-compassion and resilience. By bringing focused awareness to the present moment without judgment, mindfulness helps us observe our thoughts and emotions with greater clarity and equanimity. Through regular meditation practice, we can develop a greater sense of self-awareness and self-acceptance, allowing us to respond to challenges with compassion and resilience rather than reactively.

Moreover, reframing negative self-talk is essential for building inner strength and resilience. Often, our inner critic can be our harshest adversary, undermining our confidence and self-worth with relentless criticism and self-doubt. By challenging negative self-talk and replacing it with more compassionate and empowering language, we can cultivate a greater sense of self-compassion and resilience. For example, instead of saying "I'm not good enough," we can reframe it as "I am worthy of love and acceptance just as I am."

Ultimately, cultivating self-compassion and resilience is a lifelong journey—one that requires patience, practice, and self-reflection. By incorporating self-care rituals, self-affirmations, mindfulness meditation, and positive self-talk into our daily lives, we can nurture our inner strength and resilience, allowing us to navigate life's challenges with grace and compassion. So the next time you find yourself facing adversity, remember to treat yourself with kindness, embrace your imperfections, and trust in your ability to overcome any obstacle that comes your way.

Building resilience and cultivating self-compassion isn't just about weathering the storms of life; it's also about fostering a deeper sense of connection and empathy with ourselves and others. When we extend compassion to ourselves, we become more attuned to the suffering and struggles of those around us, fostering greater empathy and understanding in our relationships. This interconnectedness reminds us that we are not alone in our struggles and that compassion is a powerful force for healing and transformation.

Furthermore, practicing gratitude can be a powerful antidote to adversity, helping to shift our focus from what is lacking to what is present and meaningful in our lives. By consciously cultivating gratitude for the blessings, big and small, we can reframe our perspective and cultivate a sense of abundance and resilience. Whether it's expressing gratitude for the support of loved ones, the beauty of nature, or the simple joys of everyday life, gratitude reminds us of the inherent goodness and resilience within ourselves and the world around us.

Moreover, embracing vulnerability is essential for building resilience and fostering self-compassion. Contrary to popular belief, vulnerability is not a sign of weakness but rather a courageous act of authenticity and self-expression. When we allow ourselves to be vulnerable—to acknowledge our fears, insecurities, and imperfections—we create space for connection, growth, and healing. By embracing vulnerability with compassion and self-acceptance, we can transform our struggles into sources of strength and resilience.

In conclusion, cultivating self-compassion and resilience is a journey of self-discovery and growth—one that requires courage, patience, and commitment. By incorporating practices such as self-care, self-affirmations, mindfulness meditation, and gratitude into our daily lives, we can nurture our inner strength and resilience, allowing us to navigate life's challenges with grace and compassion. So the next time you find yourself facing adversity, remember to treat yourself with kindness, embrace your vulnerabilities, and trust in your ability to rise above life's challenges with courage and resilience.

Chapter 9: Manifestation in Relationships and Health

In this chapter, we delve into two vital aspects of our lives: relationships and health. Relationships form the cornerstone of our social connections, while health underpins our overall well-being and vitality. By harnessing the principles of manifestation, we have the opportunity to cultivate deeper connections in our relationships and enhance our physical and emotional health.

Manifestation principles are not confined to material possessions or external achievements; they extend to every facet of our existence, including the intricate tapestry of our relationships and the temple of our physical bodies. As we explore the application of manifestation in relationships and health, we embark on a transformative journey of self-discovery, growth, and fulfilment.

Through this chapter, we will unravel the mysteries of how our thoughts, beliefs, and intentions shape the dynamics of our relationships and influence our health outcomes. We will uncover practical strategies, timeless wisdom, and empowering practices that empower us to manifest greater harmony, love, and well-being in our lives.

Join us as we unlock the power of manifestation to nurture thriving relationships, cultivate vibrant health, and embark on a journey of holistic transformation. Together, let us embrace the profound potential within us to create the lives we truly desire, filled with love, vitality, and abundance.

Manifestation Principles in Relationships

In the realm of relationships, the concept of manifestation holds profound significance, offering insights into the dynamics of attraction, connection, and fulfilment. At its core, manifestation in relationships revolves around the principle that our beliefs, intentions, and energy play a pivotal role in shaping the quality of our interactions and the people we draw into our lives. By understanding and harnessing these manifestation principles, we can cultivate harmonious and fulfilling relationships that align with our deepest desires and intentions.

Beliefs serve as the foundation upon which our experiences in relationships are built. Our beliefs about love, worthiness, and compatibility shape the way we perceive ourselves and others, influencing the types of relationships we attract and the dynamics that unfold within them. If we hold limiting beliefs about our deservingness of love or the availability of compatible partners, we inadvertently repel opportunities for meaningful connections. Therefore, a crucial aspect of manifestation in relationships involves identifying and transforming limiting beliefs into empowering ones that affirm our worthiness of love and our capacity to cultivate fulfilling relationships.

Intentions are another key ingredient in the manifestation process, serving as the guiding force behind our desires and aspirations in relationships. When we set clear and aligned intentions for the type of relationship we wish to manifest, we signal to the universe our readiness to receive and cultivate that experience. Intentions act as a beacon, drawing towards us individuals and opportunities that resonate with our vision for love and connection. By consciously clarifying and affirming our intentions, we activate the manifestation process and invite the fulfilment of our desires into our lives.

Energy is the subtle yet potent force that underlies all manifestations in relationships. Our thoughts, emotions, and vibrational frequency emit energetic signals that attract and repel people and experiences into our reality. Positive, high-vibrational energy magnetizes harmonious and uplifting relationships, while negative, low-vibrational energy can repel love and create discord within existing relationships. Therefore, cultivating positive energy through practices such as gratitude, self-love, and mindfulness is essential for manifesting and maintaining healthy, fulfilling relationships.

Practical techniques for manifesting harmonious and fulfilling relationships abound, offering individuals tangible tools for aligning their beliefs, intentions, and energy with their desired relationship outcomes. Visualization, for example, allows individuals to vividly imagine and embody the feelings and experiences associated with their ideal relationships, thereby amplifying the manifestation process. Affirmations serve as powerful statements of intention, reinforcing positive beliefs and aligning the subconscious mind with the desired relationship outcomes. Additionally, taking inspired action, such as actively participating in social activities, pursuing hobbies, or joining interest groups, can create opportunities for serendipitous encounters and meaningful connections.

In essence, manifestation principles offer a transformative framework for understanding and cultivating fulfilling relationships. By consciously aligning our beliefs, intentions, and energy with our deepest desires, we can attract and nurture connections that bring joy, fulfilment, and growth into our lives. Through practical techniques and intentional practices, we empower ourselves to co-create the loving and supportive relationships we truly deserve.

Manifesting Health and Well-being

Manifestation principles extend far beyond the realm of material desires, encompassing every aspect of our lives, including health and well-being. At its core, manifestation in the context of health acknowledges the profound connection between the mind and body, recognizing that our thoughts, beliefs, and energy play a significant role in shaping our physical health and overall well-being. By harnessing the power of manifestation, individuals can proactively cultivate improved health, vitality, and resilience, thereby enhancing their quality of life and sense of fulfilment.

The mind-body connection serves as the cornerstone of manifestation for improved health and well-being. Research in the field of psychoneuroimmunology has demonstrated the intricate interplay between mental states, emotional experiences, and physiological responses within the body. Our thoughts, beliefs, and emotions can profoundly impact the functioning of our immune system, nervous system, and hormonal balance, influencing everything from our susceptibility to illness to our capacity for healing and recovery. Therefore, cultivating a positive mindset, nurturing emotional well-being, and managing stress effectively are essential components of manifesting optimal health and vitality.

Strategies for manifesting improved health and well-being encompass a holistic approach that addresses the interconnectedness of mind, body, and spirit. Practicing mindfulness and meditation, for example, allows individuals to cultivate present-moment awareness and cultivate a sense of inner peace and equilibrium. By quieting the chatter of the mind and attuning to the wisdom of the body, individuals can reduce stress, alleviate anxiety, and enhance their overall sense of well-being. Additionally, adopting healthy lifestyle habits, such as regular exercise, nutritious eating, and restorative sleep, provides a solid foundation for physical health and vitality.

Moreover, the power of visualization and positive affirmations can be harnessed to manifest specific health outcomes and desired states of well-being. Through the practice of visualization, individuals can mentally rehearse and embody the experience of being healthy, vibrant, and energetic, thereby priming their subconscious mind to support the manifestation of those outcomes in reality. Similarly, affirmations serve as potent statements of intention that reinforce positive beliefs about health and well-being, reprogramming the subconscious mind for success and resilience.

Furthermore, fostering a sense of gratitude and appreciation for the body's innate wisdom and healing capacity can amplify the manifestation process and cultivate a deeper sense of well-being. By expressing gratitude for the body's resilience, vitality, and capacity for renewal, individuals can shift their focus from perceived limitations to the boundless potential for health and healing within themselves. Gratitude practices, such as keeping a gratitude journal or engaging in daily reflections, serve as powerful reminders of the abundance of blessings and opportunities for growth present in every moment.

In essence, manifestation principles offer a transformative framework for enhancing health and well-being from the inside out. By cultivating a positive mindset, nurturing emotional well-being, and adopting healthy lifestyle habits, individuals can harness the power of their thoughts, beliefs, and energy to manifest optimal health, vitality, and resilience. Through the practice of visualization, positive affirmations, and gratitude, individuals can align their intentions with their deepest desires and co-create a life of vibrant health and well-being.

Tips for Attracting Positive Relationships and Good Health

In the pursuit of a fulfilling life, positive relationships and good health are foundational pillars that contribute to our overall well-being and happiness. Manifestation principles offer valuable insights and techniques for attracting and nurturing these essential elements, empowering individuals to cultivate thriving relationships and vibrant health. By incorporating self-love, self-care, and intentional practices into their daily lives, individuals can harness the power of manifestation to manifest positive relationships and maintain optimal health and vitality.

Attracting positive and fulfilling relationships begins with cultivating a deep sense of self-love and self-worth. When we prioritize our own well-being and happiness, we naturally radiate an aura of confidence and authenticity that attracts like-minded individuals into our lives. Practicing self-love involves nurturing a compassionate and nurturing relationship with ourselves, embracing our strengths, flaws, and unique qualities with acceptance and appreciation. By recognizing and honoring our own worthiness of love and respect, we set the stage for attracting relationships that uplift and support us on our journey.

Self-care is another essential component of fostering healthy relationships, as it ensures that we are meeting our own needs and maintaining balance in our lives. Setting aside time for activities that nourish our body, mind, and spirit—such as exercise, meditation, creative expression, and time in nature—helps us recharge our energy reserves and cultivate a sense of inner peace and vitality. Additionally, setting boundaries is crucial for maintaining healthy relationships, as it allows us to protect our emotional well-being and communicate our needs and preferences effectively. By establishing clear boundaries and asserting our needs with love and respect, we create space for authentic connection and mutual respect in our relationships.

In addition to nurturing positive relationships, manifestation principles can also be applied to maintain good health and vitality. The mind-body connection plays a significant role in our overall well-being, as our thoughts, beliefs, and emotions can impact our physical health and resilience. Therefore, cultivating a positive mindset and adopting practices that promote emotional balance and stress management—such as mindfulness, gratitude, and positive affirmations—is essential for supporting optimal health and vitality. By focusing on thoughts and beliefs that align with health and vitality, individuals can harness the power of manifestation to manifest their desired health outcomes and overcome challenges with resilience.

Furthermore, maintaining good health and vitality through manifestation principles involves adopting lifestyle habits that support holistic well-being. Regular exercise, nutritious eating, adequate sleep, and stress reduction techniques—such as deep breathing, relaxation exercises, and spending time in nature—help to optimize physical health and energy levels. Additionally, fostering a sense of gratitude and appreciation for the body's innate wisdom and healing capacity can amplify the manifestation process and promote a deeper sense of well-being. By expressing gratitude for the body's resilience, vitality, and capacity for renewal, individuals can cultivate a positive outlook on their health and well-being, inspiring them to take proactive steps towards their health goals.

In conclusion, attracting positive relationships and good health through manifestation principles is a journey of self-discovery and empowerment. By prioritizing self-love, self-care, and setting boundaries in relationships, individuals can create a supportive and nurturing environment that fosters authentic connection and mutual respect. Likewise, by adopting practices that promote emotional balance and stress management, individuals can maintain optimal health and vitality through the power of their thoughts and beliefs. Through intentional practices and lifestyle habits that align with their deepest desires, individuals can radiate positivity and thrive in both their relationships and their health.

Chapter 10: Manifesting Abundance and Success

In this pivotal chapter, we embark on a profound exploration of the principles, practices, and mindset shifts that pave the path to abundance and success in every aspect of our lives. From financial prosperity to career fulfilment, from health and well-being to opportunities and wealth, we delve into the limitless possibilities of manifestation and unlock the secrets to realizing our deepest aspirations.

Manifestation is the art of consciously creating our reality, sculpting our destinies with intention, belief, and aligned action. In this chapter, we illuminate the path to abundance and success, unveiling the transformative potential within each of us to manifest our dreams into reality. Whether you seek financial freedom, career advancement, vibrant health, or abundant opportunities, the principles of manifestation offer a guiding light to navigate the journey towards your goals.

In the pursuit of abundance and success, we traverse diverse pathways, each offering unique insights and opportunities for growth. From manifesting financial abundance to cultivating a thriving career, from attracting opportunities to fostering well-being, we explore the multifaceted dimensions of abundance and success. Through practical strategies, empowering techniques, and inspiring stories, we illuminate the way forward, empowering you to unleash your potential and manifest the life of your dreams.

At the heart of manifesting abundance and success lies the cultivation of an abundance mindset—a way of thinking and being that embraces the limitless potential of the universe. Through gratitude, positivity, and unwavering belief in your ability to manifest your desires, you awaken the dormant forces within you to attract wealth, opportunities, and prosperity into your life. In this chapter, we delve into the transformative power of an abundance mindset, offering tools and practices to anchor yourself in a state of abundance and unleash the boundless creativity and potential that resides within you.

As you embark on this chapter of your journey, I invite you to open your heart and mind to the infinite possibilities that await you. With courage, intention, and unwavering faith in your ability to manifest abundance and success, you step into the realm of limitless potentiality—a realm where dreams take flight, aspirations become reality, and every moment is infused with the magic of creation. Together, let us unlock the doors to abundance and success, and pave the way for a future filled with prosperity, joy, and fulfilment.

Unleashing Financial Prosperity

In the grand tapestry of life, financial abundance stands as a vital thread, weaving together our aspirations, dreams, and desires into a fabric of prosperity and opportunity. Yet, for many, the journey towards financial abundance remains elusive, shrouded in uncertainty and doubt. How can one navigate the labyrinth of economic challenges and emerge victorious, basking in the glow of financial prosperity? The answer lies in the transformative power of manifestation—an ancient art form that empowers individuals to sculpt their financial destinies with intention, belief, and aligned action.

Financial abundance manifestation is more than a mere exercise in wishful thinking; it is a deliberate and conscious process of aligning one's thoughts, beliefs, and actions with the vibration of wealth and prosperity. At its core, financial abundance manifestation recognizes the inherent abundance of the universe and our innate capacity to attract wealth and abundance into our lives. By harnessing the principles of manifestation, individuals can unlock the doors to financial prosperity and pave the way for a future filled with abundance and success.

At the heart of financial abundance manifestation lies a deep understanding of the principles of abundance and wealth attraction. Central to these principles is the law of attraction—the belief that like attracts like and that our thoughts and beliefs shape our reality. When we align our thoughts and beliefs with the vibration of abundance, we create a magnetic field that draws wealth and prosperity into our lives. Additionally, the principle of gratitude plays a pivotal role in wealth attraction, as expressing gratitude for our current financial situation opens the doors to even greater abundance.

Manifesting financial prosperity requires a multifaceted approach that incorporates a variety of practical techniques and strategies. Visualization, for example, is a powerful tool for manifesting financial abundance. By vividly imagining oneself living a life of financial freedom and prosperity, individuals can program their subconscious minds to attract wealth and abundance into their lives. Similarly, affirmations—positive statements repeated regularly—can rewire the subconscious mind for success and abundance, instilling a sense of confidence and belief in one's ability to attract wealth.

In addition to visualization and affirmations, gratitude practices play a crucial role in manifesting financial prosperity. By expressing gratitude for the wealth and abundance already present in one's life, individuals create a fertile ground for the seeds of future prosperity to take root and flourish. Moreover, taking inspired action towards one's financial goals is essential for manifestation success. Whether it's investing in education and skill development, seizing new opportunities, or pursuing entrepreneurial ventures, action is the catalyst that transforms dreams into reality.

Manifesting financial abundance is not merely a matter of luck or chance; it is a deliberate and conscious process of aligning one's thoughts, beliefs, and actions with the vibration of wealth and prosperity. By understanding the principles of abundance and wealth attraction and implementing practical techniques such as visualization, affirmations, and gratitude practices, individuals can unlock the doors to financial prosperity and pave the way for a future filled with abundance and success.

Strategies for Success in the Modern Professional Landscape

In the dynamic landscape of professional endeavors, the pursuit of career and business success is often marked by twists and turns, challenges, and triumphs. While traditional approaches to career advancement and entrepreneurial ventures emphasize hard work and strategic planning, there exists a transformative pathway that transcends conventional wisdom—the art of manifestation. In this comprehensive exploration, we delve into the intersection of manifestation and professional success, unveiling strategies, techniques, and insights to propel individuals towards their career and business aspirations.

At its essence, manifestation is the process of bringing one's desires and intentions into physical reality through focused thought, belief, and action. When applied to the realm of career and business, manifestation operates as a guiding force, shaping the trajectory of individuals' professional journeys and catalyzing the realization of their goals. By aligning their thoughts, beliefs, and actions with the vibration of success, individuals can unlock hidden potentials, attract opportunities, and overcome obstacles on the path to career and business success.

The journey towards career and business success begins with a clear vision and well-defined goals. To harness the power of manifestation in this pursuit, individuals must first articulate their aspirations and ambitions with precision and clarity. By setting specific, measurable, achievable, relevant, and time-bound (SMART) goals, individuals create a roadmap for success that is aligned with manifestation principles. Additionally, it is essential to infuse these goals with positive energy and belief, visualizing them as already accomplished and celebrating each milestone along the way.

In the pursuit of professional success, challenges and setbacks are inevitable. However, with the principles of manifestation as their guiding light, individuals can navigate these obstacles with resilience, determination, and grace. Visualization, for example, is a powerful technique for overcoming challenges, as it allows individuals to vividly imagine themselves overcoming obstacles and achieving their goals. Similarly, affirmations—positive statements repeated regularly—can reframe limiting beliefs and instill confidence in one's ability to overcome adversity.

Moreover, cultivating a mindset of abundance and gratitude is essential for resilience in the face of challenges. By focusing on the abundance already present in their lives and expressing gratitude for every opportunity, individuals can shift their perspective from scarcity to abundance, thereby attracting more success into their professional endeavors. Additionally, seeking support from mentors, coaches, and like-minded individuals can provide invaluable guidance and encouragement during challenging times.

The intersection of manifestation and career/business success offers a transformative pathway for individuals to realize their professional aspirations and goals. By aligning their thoughts, beliefs, and actions with the vibration of success, individuals can unlock hidden potentials, attract opportunities, and overcome obstacles on the path to career and business success. Through strategies for setting SMART goals, techniques for overcoming challenges, and a mindset of abundance and gratitude, individuals can unleash their full potential and create a future filled with fulfilment, prosperity, and success.

Mastering the Art of Attracting Opportunities and Wealth

In the symphony of life, opportunities and wealth play a harmonious melody, orchestrating the journey towards fulfilment and abundance. Yet, for many, the pursuit of prosperity remains an enigma—a distant dream shrouded in uncertainty and doubt. How can individuals navigate the labyrinth of possibilities and unlock the gates to wealth and opportunity? The answer lies in the transformative power of manifestation—an ancient art form that empowers individuals to sculpt their destinies with intention, belief, and aligned action. In this comprehensive exploration, we unveil the strategies for attracting opportunities and wealth, guiding individuals towards a future brimming with prosperity and success.

Attracting opportunities and wealth through manifestation is more than a mere exercise in wishful thinking; it is a deliberate and conscious process of aligning one's thoughts, beliefs, and actions with the vibration of abundance. Rooted in the principles of manifestation, this transformative journey invites individuals to cultivate a wealth mindset and abundance consciousness, thereby becoming magnets for opportunities and prosperity. By understanding the dynamics of attraction and manifestation, individuals can unlock the doors to wealth and abundance and embark on a journey of limitless possibilities.

Identifying and seizing opportunities aligned with one's goals requires a keen sense of awareness and clarity of purpose. To manifest opportunities, individuals must first define their aspirations and ambitions with precision and clarity, setting specific, measurable, achievable, relevant, and time-bound (SMART) goals. With a clear vision in mind, individuals can then cultivate a proactive mindset, actively seeking out opportunities that resonate with their goals and values.

Moreover, it is essential to remain open-minded and adaptable, recognizing that opportunities often present themselves in unexpected ways and at unforeseen times. By maintaining a flexible approach to life and embracing change, individuals can position themselves to seize opportunities as they arise, capitalizing on the moment and harnessing the power of synchronicity and serendipity.

Central to the process of attracting opportunities and wealth is the cultivation of a wealth mindset and abundance consciousness. A wealth mindset transcends mere monetary wealth; it encompasses a mindset of abundance and prosperity in all areas of life—financial, emotional, spiritual, and relational. By shifting from a mindset of scarcity to one of abundance, individuals open themselves up to the infinite possibilities of the universe, inviting prosperity to flow into their lives effortlessly.

Practical techniques for cultivating a wealth mindset include affirmations, visualization, and gratitude practices. Affirmations— positive statements repeated regularly—reprogram the subconscious mind for success and abundance, instilling a sense of confidence and belief in one's ability to attract wealth. Visualization, on the other hand, allows individuals to vividly imagine themselves living a life of abundance, thereby programming their subconscious minds to manifest their desires. Additionally, gratitude practices cultivate a mindset of appreciation for the abundance already present in one's life, creating a fertile ground for the seeds of future prosperity to take root and flourish.

Attracting opportunities and wealth through manifestation is a transformative journey that invites individuals to align their thoughts, beliefs, and actions with the vibration of abundance. By cultivating a wealth mindset and abundance consciousness, individuals can become magnets for opportunities and prosperity, unlocking the gates to a future filled with fulfilment, prosperity, and success. Through practical tips for identifying and seizing opportunities aligned with their goals, individuals can navigate the labyrinth of possibilities with clarity and purpose, capitalizing on the synchronicities and serendipities that abound in the universe.

The Manifestation Blueprint for Personal Growth and Development

In the grand tapestry of life, personal growth and development stand as the threads that weave together the fabric of our existence. It's the journey of self-discovery, expansion, and evolution that propels us towards our highest potential and deepest fulfilment. Manifestation, with its transformative power, offers a profound pathway for catalyzing this journey of growth and development. In this exploration, we embark on a quest to unlock the secrets of manifestation for personal growth and development, uncovering the keys to unleashing our innate greatness in every aspect of our lives.

Manifestation, at its core, is the art of consciously creating our reality through the power of intention, belief, and aligned action. While often associated with material desires, manifestation extends far beyond tangible possessions to encompass the realm of personal growth and development. It's about aligning with our true desires, deepest aspirations, and highest potential to catalyze profound transformation and self-discovery. By harnessing the principles of manifestation, we empower ourselves to become architects of our destiny, sculpting our lives with intention and purpose.

At the heart of manifestation for personal growth and development lies the profound journey of aligning with one's true desires. This alignment is not merely about chasing external goals or societal expectations; it's about tuning into the whispers of our soul and honoring the unique path that calls to us. When we align with our true desires, we embark on a journey of holistic growth and self-discovery that transcends the confines of societal norms and expectations. We unearth hidden facets of ourselves, confront limiting beliefs, and embrace our authentic essence with courage and conviction.

Sharing Strategies for Manifesting Personal Growth in Various Areas of Life:

Manifesting personal growth is a multifaceted endeavor that encompasses every aspect of our lives, from career and education to personal relationships and beyond. Here are some strategies for manifesting growth and development in key areas of life:

1. Career: Define your career aspirations with clarity and intention. Set goals that align with your passions, strengths, and values, and take inspired action towards their realization. Cultivate a growth mindset that embraces challenges as opportunities for learning and expansion. Network, seek mentorship, and continuously invest in your skills and knowledge to propel your career forward.

2. Education: Approach education as a lifelong journey of growth and discovery. Expand your intellectual horizons by seeking out opportunities for learning and self-improvement. Set educational goals that challenge and inspire you, whether it's pursuing further studies, acquiring new skills, or exploring new fields of knowledge. Embrace the process of learning with curiosity, enthusiasm, and a thirst for knowledge.

3.Personal Relationships: Cultivate nurturing and supportive relationships that uplift and inspire you. Set intentions for the kind of relationships you desire – ones that are built on trust, respect, and authenticity. Practice effective communication, active listening, and empathy to deepen your connections with others. Invest time and energy in fostering meaningful relationships that contribute to your growth and well-being.

As we enter on this journey of manifestation for personal growth and development, let us remember that the power to transform our lives lies within us. By aligning with our true desires, embracing growth opportunities, and taking intentional action, we unlock the door to a world of infinite possibilities and profound self-discovery.

The Transformative Power of Gratitude

In the symphony of life, gratitude serves as a harmonious melody, weaving its way through the fabric of our existence and illuminating the path to abundance and fulfilment. Rooted in the principles of manifestation, gratitude is more than a fleeting emotion or polite gesture—it is a profound state of being that catalyzes transformation, unlocks hidden potentials, and invites abundance to flow effortlessly into our lives. In this comprehensive exploration, we embark on a journey to understand the transformative power of gratitude in manifestation, exploring techniques for cultivating a mindset of abundance and uncovering the profound connection between gratitude, abundance, and overall success in life.

At its essence, gratitude is a state of appreciation and acknowledgment for the blessings, opportunities, and experiences that enrich our lives. In the realm of manifestation, gratitude serves as a potent catalyst, amplifying our vibrational frequency and aligning us with the abundance that surrounds us. By acknowledging and expressing gratitude for the abundance already present in our lives, we signal to the universe our openness to receiving more blessings and opportunities—a powerful act of co-creation that propels us towards our desired outcomes.

Moreover, gratitude has been scientifically proven to enhance overall well-being, increase resilience, and foster deeper connections with others. When we cultivate a mindset of gratitude, we shift our perspective from scarcity to abundance, thereby opening ourselves up to a world of infinite possibilities and opportunities. In essence, gratitude is the gateway to abundance—a sacred key that unlocks the treasures of the universe and invites prosperity to flow effortlessly into our lives.

Cultivating a mindset of abundance begins with a simple yet profound practice—gratitude journaling. By dedicating a few moments each day to reflect on the blessings, big and small, that grace our lives, we cultivate an attitude of appreciation that reverberates throughout our being. In addition to gratitude journaling, appreciation practices such as expressing heartfelt thanks to others, savoring life's simple pleasures, and cultivating mindfulness in daily activities further deepen our connection to abundance and amplify the manifestation process.

Furthermore, mindfulness exercises such as meditation and conscious breathing serve as powerful tools for cultivating a mindset of abundance. By anchoring our awareness in the present moment and cultivating a sense of presence and gratitude, we transcend the limitations of the egoic mind and tap into the boundless reservoir of abundance that resides within us. Through these practices, we align ourselves with the natural flow of life, allowing abundance to effortlessly unfold in every area of our lives.

The profound connection between gratitude, abundance, and overall success in life cannot be overstated. When we approach life with an attitude of gratitude, we attract more blessings, opportunities, and abundance into our lives. Moreover, gratitude serves as a powerful antidote to fear, anxiety, and scarcity thinking, allowing us to navigate life's challenges with grace and resilience.

Furthermore, studies have shown that individuals who cultivate a mindset of gratitude experience greater levels of happiness, fulfilment, and overall well-being. By acknowledging and appreciating the abundance already present in our lives, we shift our focus from what is lacking to what is abundant, thereby empowering ourselves to create more of what we desire. In essence, gratitude is the key that unlocks the door to a life of limitless abundance and success.

Cultivating a mindset of gratitude and abundance is a transformative journey that invites us to awaken to the inherent richness and blessings that surround us. By embracing gratitude as a way of life and practicing techniques such as gratitude journaling, appreciation practices, and mindfulness exercises, we align ourselves with the natural flow of abundance and invite prosperity to flow effortlessly into our lives. Through the profound connection between gratitude, abundance, and overall success in life, we unlock the doors to a future filled with joy, fulfilment, and limitless possibilities.

Chapter 11: Manifestation Rituals and Practices

In this chapter, we delve into the heart of manifestation—rituals and practices. Here, we explore the tangible methods and daily routines that empower us to align with our deepest desires, manifest our dreams, and cultivate a life of abundance and fulfilment.

Manifestation is not merely about wishing upon a star; it is a dynamic process that requires intention, action, and alignment with the universe's energy. Manifestation rituals and practices serve as our tools for harnessing this energy, guiding our intentions, and propelling us toward our desired outcomes.

Throughout this chapter, we will uncover an array of manifestation rituals, daily practices, and personal routines designed to ignite the manifestation process and infuse our lives with purpose, abundance, and joy. From morning rituals that set the tone for our day to evening practices that nurture gratitude and reflection, each ritual serves as a sacred pathway to manifestation.

Moreover, we will explore the power of personalized manifestation routines, encouraging you to craft a practice that resonates deeply with your unique desires, preferences, and aspirations. By embracing your individual journey and designing a manifestation routine tailored to your needs, you can unlock the full potential of manifestation and manifest your dreams with clarity and confidence.

So, whether you're a seasoned manifestor seeking to refine your practice or a newcomer eager to embark on this transformative journey, this chapter offers a wealth of insights, inspiration, and practical guidance to support you every step of the way. Get ready to immerse yourself in the magic of manifestation rituals and practices as we embark on this empowering exploration together.

Mastering Manifestation: A Comprehensive Guide to Daily Rituals and Practices

Introduction: In the pursuit of manifesting our dreams and desires, consistency and intentionality are key. Manifestation rituals and daily practices serve as powerful tools to align our thoughts, emotions, and actions with our deepest aspirations. By incorporating these rituals into our daily lives, we can cultivate a mindset of abundance, attract positive energy, and manifest our goals with clarity and purpose. In this article, we will explore a diverse collection of manifestation rituals and daily practices, each designed to enhance our manifestation journey and empower us to create the life we envision.

Introduction to Manifestation Rituals and Daily Practices Manifestation rituals are intentional actions or ceremonies designed to align our energy with our desires and manifest our goals into reality. These rituals are grounded in the principles of intentionality, mindfulness, and alignment with the universe's energy. Daily practices complement manifestation rituals by reinforcing positive habits and fostering a mindset of abundance.

Morning Manifestation Rituals

> Setting Intentions for the Day: Begin each morning by setting clear intentions for the day ahead. Write down your goals and desires, affirming your commitment to manifesting them.

> Visualization Exercises: Engage in visualization exercises to mentally rehearse your desired outcomes. Close your eyes and vividly imagine yourself achieving your goals, tapping into the emotions associated with success.

> Affirmations and Positive Declarations: Start your day with affirmations and positive declarations. Repeat empowering statements that affirm your worthiness, capability, and readiness to receive abundance.

Evening Manifestation Rituals

> Reflecting on the Day's Manifestations: Take time in the evening to reflect on the manifestations and synchronicities you experienced throughout the day. Express gratitude for

the blessings in your life and acknowledge the progress you've made.

Gratitude Journaling: Maintain a gratitude journal where you record three things you're grateful for each day. Cultivating an attitude of gratitude opens your heart to receive abundance and attracts more blessings into your life.

Releasing Negative Energy and Limiting Beliefs: Release negative energy and limiting beliefs through journaling or meditation. Identify any fears or doubts that arise and consciously release them, affirming your belief in your ability to manifest your desires.

Daily Manifestation Practices

Gratitude Practice: Incorporate gratitude into your daily routine by expressing appreciation for the blessings in your life. Practice gratitude through spoken or written affirmations, acknowledging the abundance that surrounds you.

Visualization Techniques: Set aside time each day for visualization exercises. Use guided imagery to visualize your goals as already accomplished, tapping into the emotions of joy, fulfilment, and gratitude.

Affirmations and Positive Self-Talk: Integrate affirmations and positive self-talk into your daily routine. Affirm your worthiness, abundance, and success, replacing negative self-talk with empowering statements.

Mindfulness and Meditation Exercises: Cultivate mindfulness and presence through meditation and mindfulness exercises. Quiet the mind, focus on the present moment, and connect with the universal energy that supports your manifestation journey.

Actively Pursuing Goals and Opportunities: Take inspired action toward your goals by actively seeking opportunities and taking steps to manifest your desires. Be proactive in pursuing your dreams and remain open to the signs and synchronicities that guide your path.

Additional Manifestation Rituals and Practices

Moon Manifestation Rituals: Harness the energy of the moon phases to amplify your manifestation efforts. Set intentions during the new moon, release what no longer serves you during the full moon, and align your actions with the lunar cycle.

Crystal Healing Practices: Incorporate crystals into your manifestation rituals to amplify your intentions and clear energetic blockages. Choose crystals that resonate with your goals and intentions, and use them during meditation or visualization exercises.

Journal Prompts and Reflection Exercises: Use journal prompts and reflection exercises to deepen your manifestation practice. Write about your goals, desires, and manifestations, and explore any resistance or limiting beliefs that arise.

Energy Clearing and Space Cleansing Techniques: Clear stagnant energy and create a supportive environment for manifestation through energy clearing and space cleansing techniques. Use tools such as sage, palo santo, or sound healing to purify your space and create a conducive atmosphere for manifestation.

Tips for Incorporating Manifestation Rituals into Daily Life

Creating a Sacred Space for Manifestation Rituals: Designate a special area in your home where you can perform your manifestation rituals and daily practices. Fill this space with items that inspire and uplift you, such as candles, crystals, or meaningful symbols.

Setting Aside Dedicated Time Each Day for Manifestation Practices: Schedule time each day to engage in manifestation rituals and practices. Whether it's in the morning, evening, or throughout the day, prioritize your manifestation journey and commit to consistency.

Staying Consistent and Committed to the Practice: Manifestation is a journey, not a destination. Stay committed to your practice even when faced with challenges or setbacks. Trust in the process and remain consistent in your efforts.

Flexibility and Adaptation Based on Individual Needs and Preferences: Tailor your manifestation rituals and practices to suit your individual needs and preferences. Experiment with different techniques and adjust your routine as needed to find what works best for you.

Manifestation rituals and daily practices are powerful tools for aligning with the energy of abundance and manifesting our desires into reality. By incorporating these practices into our daily lives, we can cultivate a mindset of gratitude, abundance, and empowerment, and manifest the life of our dreams. Whether it's through morning rituals, evening practices, or additional rituals and practices, there are endless opportunities to infuse our lives with intentionality and purpose. Remember, the key to manifestation lies in consistent practice, unwavering belief, and a willingness to embrace the journey with an open heart and mind.

Crafting Your Unique Path: Creating a Personal Manifestation Routine

Manifestation is a powerful practice that allows us to bring our desires and intentions into reality. While there are numerous manifestation techniques and rituals available, creating a personalized manifestation routine tailored to our individual needs and preferences can enhance its effectiveness. In this article, we will delve into the importance of personalized manifestation routines and provide practical guidance for readers to create their own. From self-reflection and goal setting to integrating rituals into daily life and embracing growth, this article will empower readers to embark on a journey of self-discovery and manifestation success.

Manifestation is a deeply personal journey, and no two individuals are exactly alike. Recognizing the uniqueness of our desires, goals, and circumstances is crucial in creating a manifestation routine that resonates with us. By tailoring manifestation practices to align with our personal preferences and needs, we can ensure that our routine feels authentic and meaningful.

Before embarking on our manifestation journey, it's essential to engage in self-reflection and identify our core desires and intentions. By clarifying what we truly want to manifest in our lives, we can set specific, achievable goals that serve as the foundation for our manifestation practice. Setting clear intentions allows us to focus our energy and attention on what matters most to us.

There are countless manifestation techniques and rituals available, each with its own unique benefits and applications. From visualization and affirmations to scripting and gratitude practices, it's essential to research and experiment with various techniques to find what resonates best with us. By evaluating the effectiveness of different techniques, we can identify those that align most closely with our goals and preferences.

Once we have explored different manifestation techniques, it's time to design our personal manifestation routine. This involves selecting preferred practices and rituals that feel most authentic and impactful to us. Whether it's creating a daily or weekly schedule for manifestation activities or incorporating flexibility and adaptability into our routine, the key is to design a practice that feels sustainable and aligned with our lifestyle.

Incorporating manifestation rituals into our daily life is essential for maintaining consistency and momentum in our practice. Finding balance between manifestation practices and other commitments ensures that we can prioritize our goals while still attending to our responsibilities. Creating reminders and cues to reinforce our manifestation routine helps us stay on track and maintain focus, while making adjustments based on feedback and progress allows us to fine-tune our practice over time.

As we progress on our manifestation journey, it's important to embrace evolution and growth. Allowing our manifestation routine to evolve over time ensures that it remains aligned with our changing desires and circumstances. Embracing challenges and setbacks as opportunities for growth allows us to learn and adapt, while celebrating successes and milestones along the way keeps us motivated and inspired.

Seeking support from mentors, peers, or communities can provide valuable guidance and encouragement on our manifestation journey. Sharing experiences and insights with others fosters a sense of connection and solidarity, while providing encouragement and motivation to stay committed to our practice helps us overcome obstacles and persevere in the face of challenges.

Creating a personal manifestation routine is a transformative and empowering process that allows us to align with our deepest desires and manifest the life of our dreams. By understanding the importance of personalization, engaging in self-reflection and goal setting, exploring different techniques, and integrating rituals into our daily lives, we can unlock our full potential and manifest abundance, joy, and fulfilment. Remember, the power to manifest lies within us, and by crafting a personalized manifestation routine, we can harness that power to create the life we truly desire.

Harnessing Lunar Energy: The Art of Moon Manifestation Rituals

Throughout history, humans have looked to the moon with reverence, recognizing its profound influence on the natural world and our lives. In recent years, the practice of moon manifestation rituals has gained popularity as people seek to align with the cycles of the moon to manifest their desires and intentions. In this article, we will explore the power of moon manifestation rituals, delving into the significance of lunar cycles and offering practical tips for harnessing the energy of the moon for intention setting, releasing, and manifesting desires.

The moon, with its ever-changing phases, serves as a potent symbol of transformation and renewal. Each phase of the lunar cycle carries its own unique energy, offering opportunities for introspection, growth, and manifestation. By understanding the significance of lunar cycles, we can tap into the rhythm of nature and align our manifestation efforts with the cosmic forces at play.

The new moon marks the beginning of the lunar cycle, symbolizing new beginnings and fresh starts. During this phase, the moon is not visible in the sky, making it an opportune time for introspection and intention setting. To harness the energy of the new moon for manifestation, create a sacred space for reflection and journaling. Set clear, specific intentions for what you wish to manifest in the coming lunar cycle, infusing your intentions with passion and purpose.

As the moon reaches its full illumination, it symbolizes completion and culmination. The full moon is a powerful time for releasing what no longer serves us, whether it be limiting beliefs, negative emotions, or outdated patterns. To harness the energy of the full moon for manifestation, engage in rituals such as burning ceremonies, where you symbolically release what you wish to let go of into the flames. Use this time to forgive yourself and others, allowing space for new blessings to enter your life.

During the waxing phase of the lunar cycle, the moon grows in illumination, symbolizing expansion and growth. This is an ideal time for actively manifesting your desires and goals. To harness the energy of the waxing moon for manifestation, engage in visualization exercises, affirmations, and goal-setting practices. Visualize your desires as already manifested, feeling the emotions associated with their attainment. Take inspired action towards your goals, trusting that the universe will support your efforts.

As the moon wanes in illumination, it invites us to turn inward and reflect on our journey. The waning phase of the lunar cycle is a time for gratitude and introspection, allowing us to acknowledge our progress and express appreciation for our blessings. To harness the energy of the waning moon for manifestation, engage in gratitude practices such as gratitude journaling or meditation. Reflect on the abundance in your life and express gratitude for all that you have manifested thus far.

Practical Tips for Moon Manifestation Rituals:

> Create a sacred space for your rituals, free from distractions and interruptions.
>
> Use moon-related tools such as crystals, candles, or essential oils to enhance your rituals.
>
> Set clear intentions before each ritual, focusing on what you wish to manifest or release.
>
> Practice consistency by performing rituals regularly, preferably aligned with the phases of the moon.
>
> Trust in the process and remain open to receiving the blessings and opportunities that come your way.

Moon manifestation rituals offer a powerful way to align with the natural rhythms of the universe and manifest our desires. By understanding the significance of lunar cycles and harnessing the energy of the moon for intention setting, releasing, and manifesting, we can tap into our innate creative power and bring our dreams to fruition. Whether you're setting intentions with the new moon, releasing with the full moon, manifesting with the waxing moon, or reflecting with the waning moon, may your moon manifestation rituals bring you closer to your heart's desires.

Amplifying Your Intentions with Crystal Healing Practices

In recent years, the use of crystals as tools for manifestation has surged in popularity as individuals seek to harness their energy to amplify intentions, enhance intuition, and support spiritual growth. Crystals, with their unique vibrational frequencies and properties, have long been revered for their healing abilities and metaphysical properties. In this article, we will explore the integration of crystal healing practices into manifestation, delving into the different types of crystals, their properties, and how to incorporate them into manifestation rituals and practices.

Crystals are natural conductors of energy, capable of absorbing, storing, and transmitting vibrational frequencies. Each crystal possesses its own unique energy signature and metaphysical properties, making them powerful allies in the manifestation process. By aligning with the energy of specific crystals, we can amplify our intentions, deepen our intuition, and accelerate our manifestation efforts.

There is a vast array of crystals available, each with its own distinct properties and associations. Some crystals are known for their ability to enhance abundance and prosperity, while others may support emotional healing or spiritual growth. Common manifestation crystals include clear quartz, known as the "master healer," which amplifies intention and clarity of thought, citrine, a stone of abundance and manifestation, and amethyst, which enhances intuition and spiritual connection. By exploring the properties of different crystals, we can choose those that resonate most strongly with our intentions and goals.

There are numerous ways to incorporate crystals into manifestation rituals and practices, allowing us to harness their energy and amplify our intentions. One common practice is to create a crystal grid, where crystals are arranged in a specific geometric pattern to amplify intention and manifestation energy. Another method is to carry or wear crystals as talismans or jewelry, keeping their energy close throughout the day. Additionally, crystals can be placed on altars or meditation spaces, infused with intention during meditation or visualization practices, or used to charge water or other objects with manifestation energy.

Practical Tips for Working with Crystals in Manifestation:

> Choose crystals that resonate with your intentions and goals, trusting your intuition to guide you to the right stones.

> Cleanse and charge your crystals regularly to clear away any stagnant energy and amplify their vibration.

> Program your crystals with specific intentions by holding them in your hands and infusing them with your desired outcome.

> Create a sacred space for your manifestation rituals, incorporating crystals, candles, and other sacred objects to enhance the energy of the space.

> Trust in the process and remain open to receiving the guidance and support that crystals offer on your manifestation journey.

Integrating crystal healing practices into manifestation can amplify our intentions, deepen our intuition, and support our spiritual growth. By understanding the properties of different crystals and how to incorporate them into manifestation rituals and practices, we can tap into their innate energy and align with our highest intentions. Whether you're creating a crystal grid, wearing crystals as talismans, or meditating with crystals to amplify intention, may your crystal manifestation practices bring you closer to your dreams and desires.

Chapter 12: Living a Manifested Life

As we journey through the culmination of this book, we find ourselves at a pivotal moment where theory transforms into practice, and aspirations take shape into reality. Throughout the preceding chapters, we've delved into the intricacies of manifestation, exploring its principles, techniques, and applications. Now, in this concluding chapter, we embark on a reflective voyage, synthesizing the essence of our exploration and ushering forth a newfound understanding of what it truly means to live a manifested life.

Manifestation is not merely a concept to be understood; it is a way of life to be embraced fully and integrated into every aspect of our being. It is about aligning our thoughts, beliefs, and actions with our deepest desires and allowing the universe to conspire in our favor. In this chapter, we summarize the key concepts that have guided our journey thus far, drawing upon the wisdom gleaned from each chapter to illuminate the path ahead.

But beyond the theoretical framework lies the heart of manifestation—the stories of individuals like you, dear reader, who have embarked on their own manifestation journeys and emerged victorious. Through shared narratives of triumph and transformation, we witness the tangible impact of manifestation principles in real lives, reinforcing our belief in the boundless potential that resides within each of us.

As we navigate through this final chapter, let us not only reflect on the past but also look to the future with unwavering optimism and determination. For the journey of manifestation is not confined to the pages of this book; it is a lifelong odyssey of self-discovery and empowerment. Let us embrace this chapter as a catalyst for continued growth and evolution, knowing that the power to manifest our dreams lies within our grasp.

So, dear reader, I invite you to immerse yourself in the pages that follow, to glean wisdom from the experiences shared, and to embark on your own journey of living a manifested life. Together, let us step boldly into the realm of endless possibilities, where dreams are realized, and destinies are fulfilled.

Throughout the book, the overarching theme revolves around the power of intention, belief, and alignment in manifesting desires. By understanding and applying these key concepts, readers are empowered to embark on their own journey of living a manifested life, where dreams become realities. Few key takeaways from this book are

Understanding Manifestation: The book delves into the fundamental principles of manifestation, elucidating how thoughts, beliefs, and emotions shape our reality. It emphasizes the power of intention and the role of the subconscious mind in manifesting desires.

Belief Systems and Perception: The book explores how our belief systems influence our perceptions of reality and shape our ability to manifest. It highlights the concept of the "belief-achievement gap" and offers insights into overcoming limiting beliefs.

Visualization and Affirmation: Visualization techniques and affirmations are presented as potent tools for manifesting desires. The book provides practical exercises and guidance on how to harness the power of visualization and affirmation to align with desired outcomes.

Self-Limiting Beliefs and Resilience: It discusses common self-limiting beliefs that hinder manifestation and offers strategies for overcoming them. The importance of resilience in persisting through challenges and setbacks is emphasized, along with techniques for cultivating resilience.

Alignment and Inspired Action: The book underscores the significance of aligning beliefs, thoughts, emotions, and actions with desired outcomes. It explores the concept of inspired action versus random effort and offers strategies for taking consistent steps toward goals.

The Law of Detachment: The chapter elucidates the concept of detachment in manifestation, emphasizing the importance of releasing attachment to specific outcomes and surrendering to the flow of life.

Manifestation in Relationships and Health: The book extends manifestation principles to relationships and health, discussing how aligning with intentions can foster abundance and well-being in these areas.

Manifesting Abundance and Success: It explores manifestation in the context of finances, career, and business success, offering strategies for attracting opportunities and wealth.

Manifestation Rituals and Practices: The chapter delves into various manifestation rituals and daily practices, encouraging readers to create personalized routines aligned with their goals and preferences.

Living a Manifested Life: The concluding chapter summarizes key concepts from the book, shares success stories of readers who have manifested their desires, and encourages readers to continue their manifestation journey with optimism and determination.

Embarking on a manifestation journey is like setting sail on a voyage towards your deepest desires and wildest dreams. It's a journey filled with twists and turns, ups and downs, but one that holds the promise of transformation and fulfilment. As you navigate through the pages of life, it's essential to keep the flame of manifestation burning bright, continuing to manifest your desires with unwavering determination and belief. In this article, we'll explore the importance of staying committed to your manifestation journey, providing insights and practical tips to keep you inspired along the way.

Take a moment to reflect on how far you've come since you began your manifestation journey. Celebrate your successes, no matter how small, and acknowledge the growth and changes you've experienced along the way. Reflecting on your progress can reignite your motivation and remind you of the power of manifestation in shaping your reality.

Reconnect with the reasons why you embarked on this manifestation journey in the first place. What are your deepest desires and aspirations? What drives you to continue manifesting? By reconnecting with your why, you can reignite your passion and purpose, fueling your determination to persist in the face of challenges.

In the midst of life's distractions and challenges, it's easy to lose sight of your intentions. Stay aligned with your desires by regularly revisiting your intentions and reaffirming your commitment to manifesting them. Practice visualization, affirmations, and other manifestation techniques to keep your intentions clear and vivid in your mind.

Remember that manifestation is not always instantaneous. It takes time for your desires to materialize, and patience is key. Trust in the process and have faith that the universe is working in your favor, even when things seem to be moving slowly or not according to plan. Trust that everything is unfolding as it should and that the universe has your back.

Detach yourself from specific outcomes and surrender to the flow of life. Trust that the universe knows what is best for you and that your desires will manifest in divine timing. Release any resistance or attachment to how or when your desires will manifest, and instead focus on aligning with the energy of abundance and positivity.

Cultivate a mindset of gratitude and appreciation for all that you have and all that is yet to come. Gratitude is a powerful manifestation tool that can amplify the energy of abundance and attract more blessings into your life. Take time each day to express gratitude for the blessings, opportunities, and experiences that come your way.

Surround yourself with positivity and inspiration to keep your manifestation journey on track. Seek out supportive communities, books, podcasts, and mentors who uplift and encourage you on your path. Surrounding yourself with positive influences can help you stay motivated and focused on manifesting your desires.

Stay Open to Possibilities: Remain open to the infinite possibilities that lie ahead on your manifestation journey. Be open to new opportunities, experiences, and pathways that may present themselves along the way. By staying open and flexible, you allow the universe to work its magic and manifest your desires in unexpected and miraculous ways.

Persist in the Face of Challenges: Challenges and setbacks are inevitable on any journey, including the manifestation journey. Instead of letting challenges deter you, see them as opportunities for growth and learning.

Persist in the face of challenges, knowing that each obstacle is a stepping stone towards the manifestation of your desires.

Trust Your Inner Guidance: Trust your intuition and inner guidance to lead you towards your desires. Your intuition is your compass, guiding you towards what is aligned with your highest good. Listen to your inner voice, follow your instincts, and trust that you are always being guided towards your manifestations.

Your manifestation journey is a lifelong odyssey filled with endless possibilities and opportunities for growth. By staying committed, aligned, and open to the magic of manifestation, you can continue to manifest your desires and live a life of abundance and fulfilment. Embrace the journey, trust the process, and never lose sight of the incredible power you hold to create the life of your dreams.

Embracing the Journey: Reflecting on the Power of Manifestation and Personal Growth

As we come to the culmination of our manifestation journey, it's essential to take a moment to reflect on the transformative path we've traveled and the incredible power of manifestation that lies within each of us. Throughout this journey, we've delved into the depths of our desires, explored manifestation techniques, and witnessed the magic of aligning our thoughts, beliefs, and actions with our dreams. Now, as we stand on the threshold of new beginnings, let's reflect on the transformational journey we've undertaken, reiterate the power of manifestation, and embrace the endless possibilities for continuous growth and personal development.

As we look back on the journey we've embarked upon, we can't help but marvel at the growth, change, and transformation we've experienced along the way. From the moment we set our intentions and took the first steps towards manifesting our desires, we've encountered challenges, celebrated successes, and discovered the power that lies within us. Each moment, each experience has been a stepping stone towards our highest potential, guiding us closer to the life we envision for ourselves.

Throughout this journey, we've learned to harness the power of manifestation to shape our reality and create the life of our dreams. We've embraced the principles of intention, belief, and alignment, understanding that our thoughts and emotions are the building blocks of our reality. We've explored manifestation techniques such as visualization, affirmations, and gratitude practices, discovering the transformative impact they have on our lives. And most importantly, we've come to realize that we hold the power to manifest our desires and create a life of abundance, joy, and fulfilment.

As we reflect on our journey, it's essential to reiterate the profound power of manifestation and the blueprint that resides within each of us. The universe is infinitely abundant, and we are co-creators of our reality. Our thoughts, beliefs, and intentions shape the world around us, influencing the circumstances, opportunities, and experiences that come into our lives. By tapping into the limitless potential within us, we can manifest our deepest desires and create a life that reflects our truest selves.

Manifestation is not just about materializing external desires; it's about aligning with our inner truth and living authentically from the inside out. It's about recognizing our worthiness, embracing abundance, and stepping into our power as conscious creators. The blueprint for our desires already exists within us; it's simply a matter of tuning in, aligning with our desires, and allowing them to unfold in divine timing.

As we continue on our manifestation journey, let's embrace the spirit of continuous growth and personal development. Manifestation is not a one-time event but a lifelong journey of self-discovery, expansion, and evolution. As we manifest our desires, we grow, change, and evolve, uncovering new layers of potential and possibility within us.

Let's commit to nurturing our personal growth and development, embracing new challenges, and stepping outside of our comfort zones. Let's cultivate a growth mindset, seeing every obstacle as an opportunity for learning and every setback as a stepping stone towards our dreams. Let's remain open to new experiences, ideas, and perspectives, knowing that growth happens when we push beyond our limits and explore the unknown.

In our journey of manifestation and personal growth, let's remember to be gentle with ourselves, to practice self-compassion, and to celebrate our progress along the way. Let's surround ourselves with a supportive community of like-minded individuals who uplift and inspire us on our journey. And most importantly, let's stay true to ourselves, honoring our deepest desires, and trusting in the wisdom of our inner guidance.

As we reflect on the transformational journey we've undertaken, let's reiterate the power of manifestation and the blueprint within us, and let's embrace the endless possibilities for continuous growth and personal development. The journey may have challenges, but it's filled with infinite opportunities for expansion, joy, and fulfilment. Let's continue manifesting our dreams, living authentically, and creating the life we desire.

About the Author

-116-

Ethan Rivers is an acclaimed author, mindfulness advocate, and dedicated teacher renowned for his transformative insights and compassionate guidance. With a profound understanding of mindfulness cultivated through years of personal practice,

Ethan empowers individuals to navigate challenges and cultivate a deep sense of presence. Through his first book, *"Mindfulness Unveiled: A Guide to Cultivating Presence and Living Fully,"* Ethan has inspired countless readers to embrace mindfulness as a pathway to inner peace and fulfilment. With his second book, Ethan continues to share his wisdom and expertise, offering readers practical tools and profound teachings to enrich their lives and deepen their connection to the present moment. Through his engaging writing style and unwavering commitment to authenticity, Ethan invites readers on a transformative journey of self-discovery, empowering them to awaken to the fullness of life's possibilities and live with greater purpose and vitality.